THIS COLORING BOOK BELONG TO:

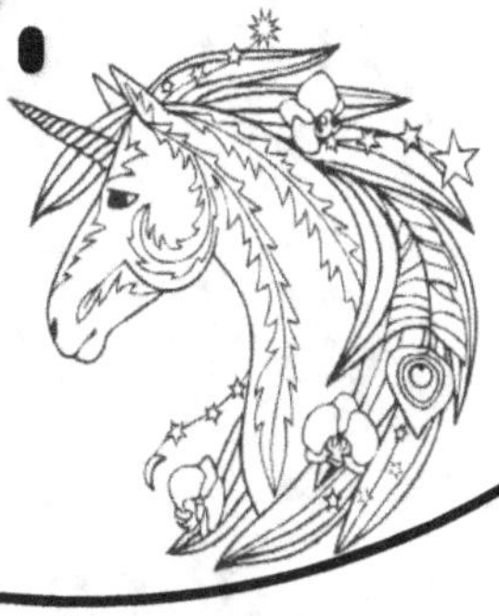

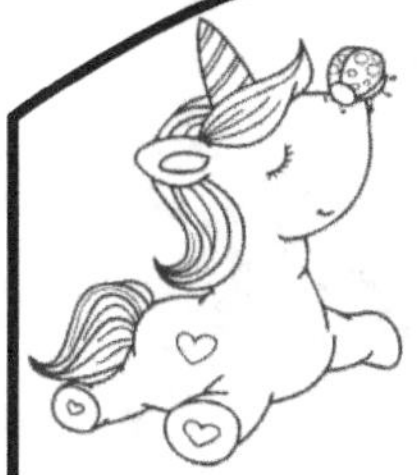

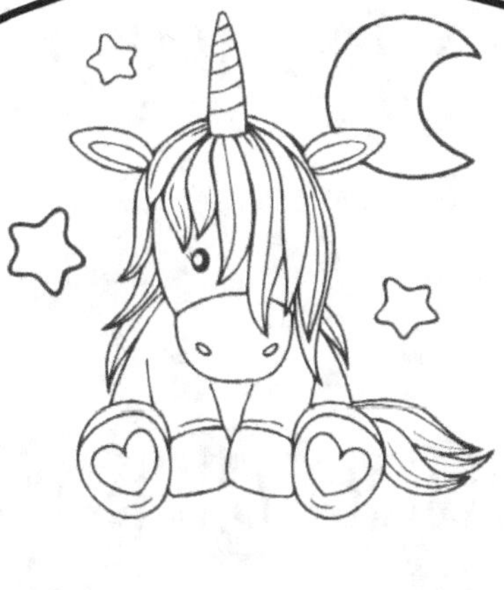

_____

This book contains positive affirmations and creative illustrations about unicorns that are a fun non-screen activity designed to build confidence and self-esteem in girls by allowing them to explore their creative side and encourages imagination.

Get a copy for all the young girls in your life.

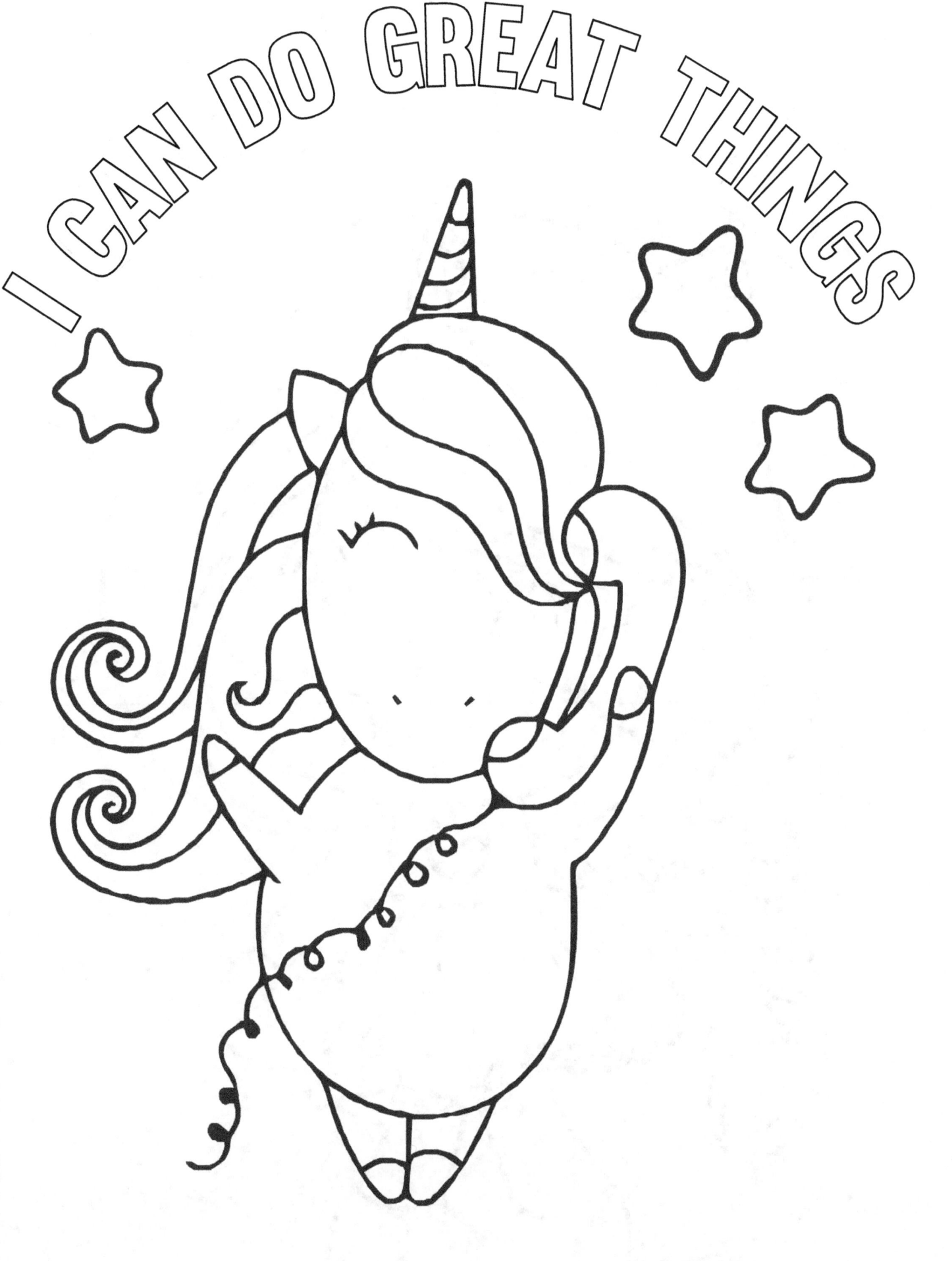

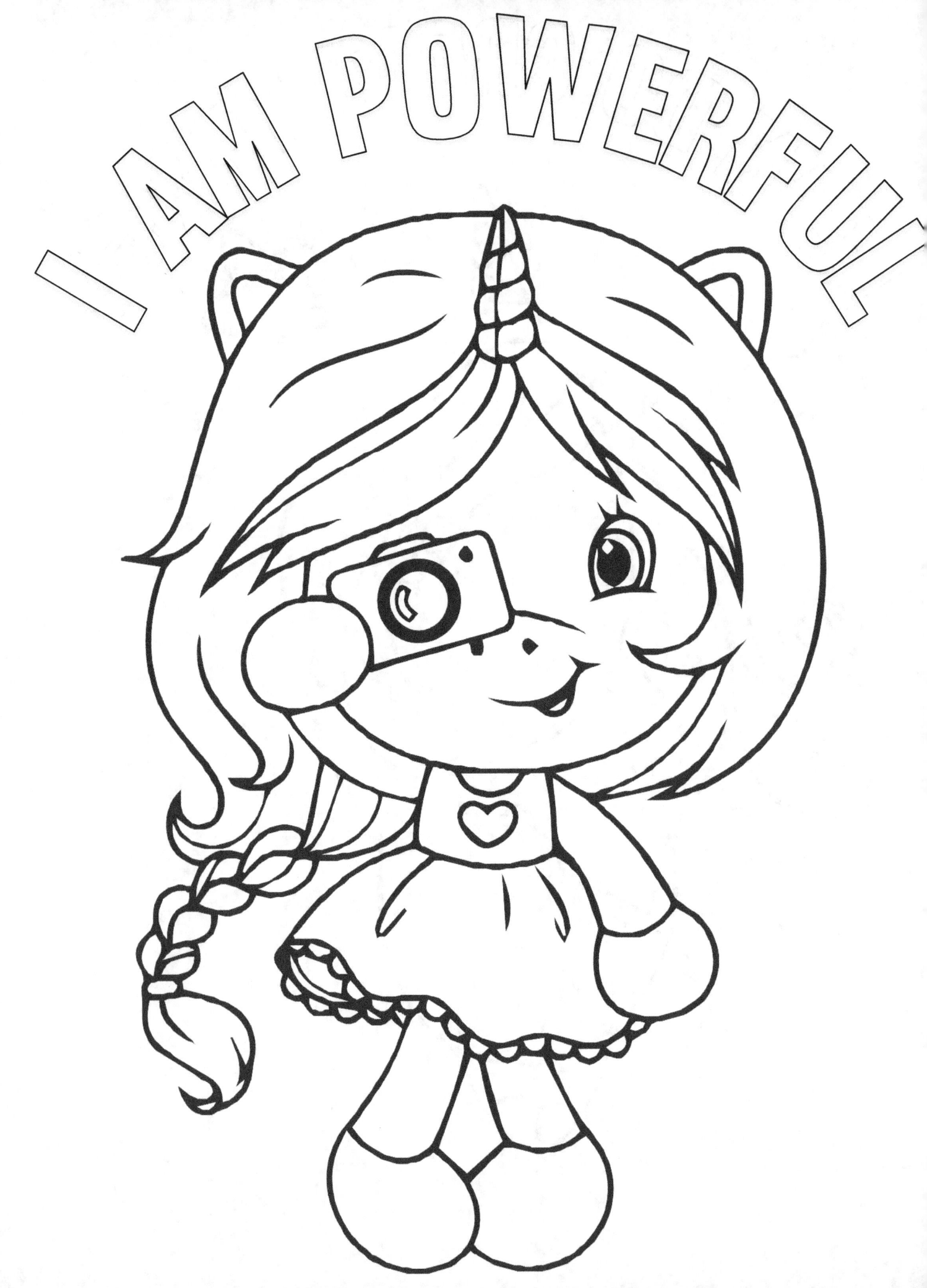

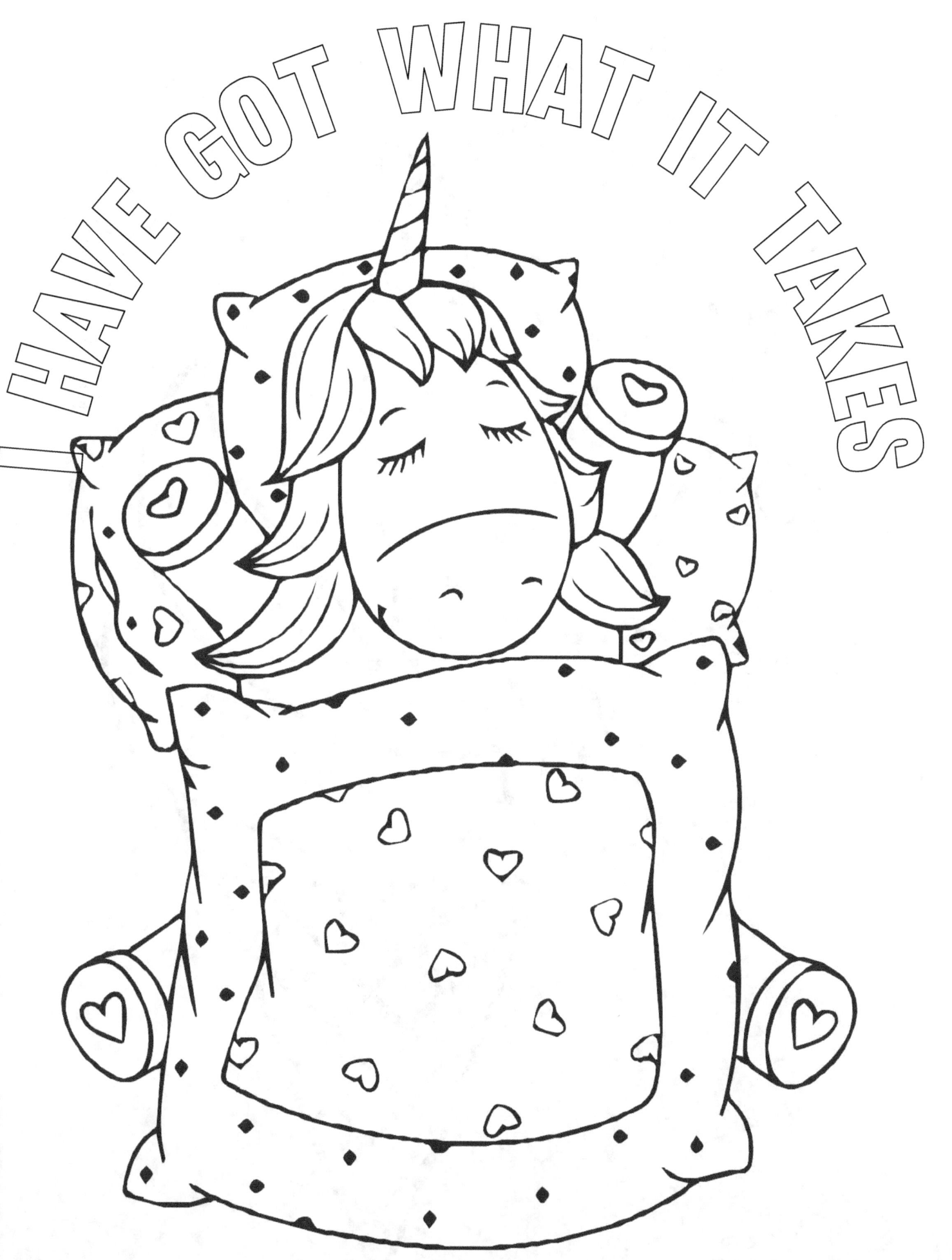

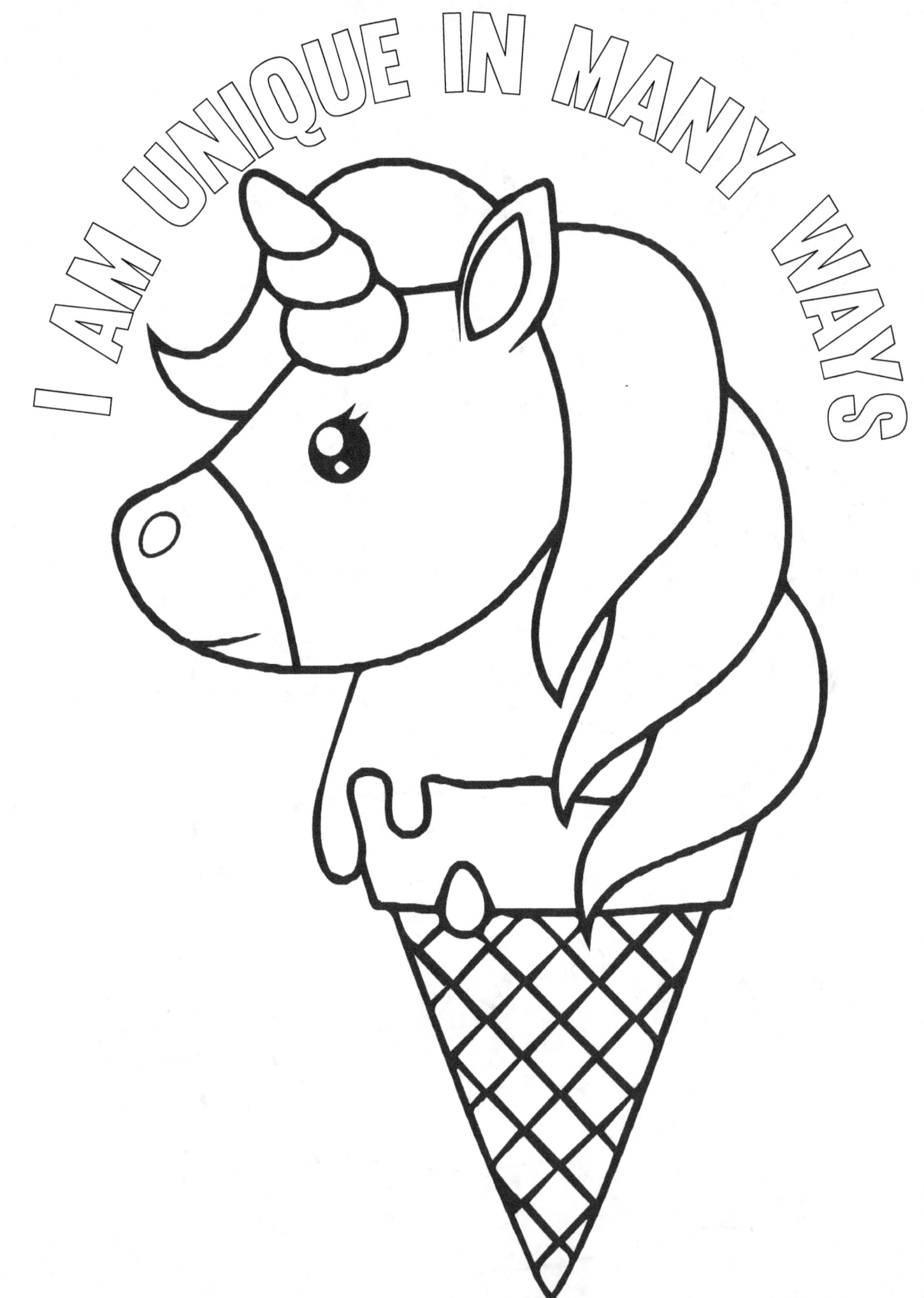

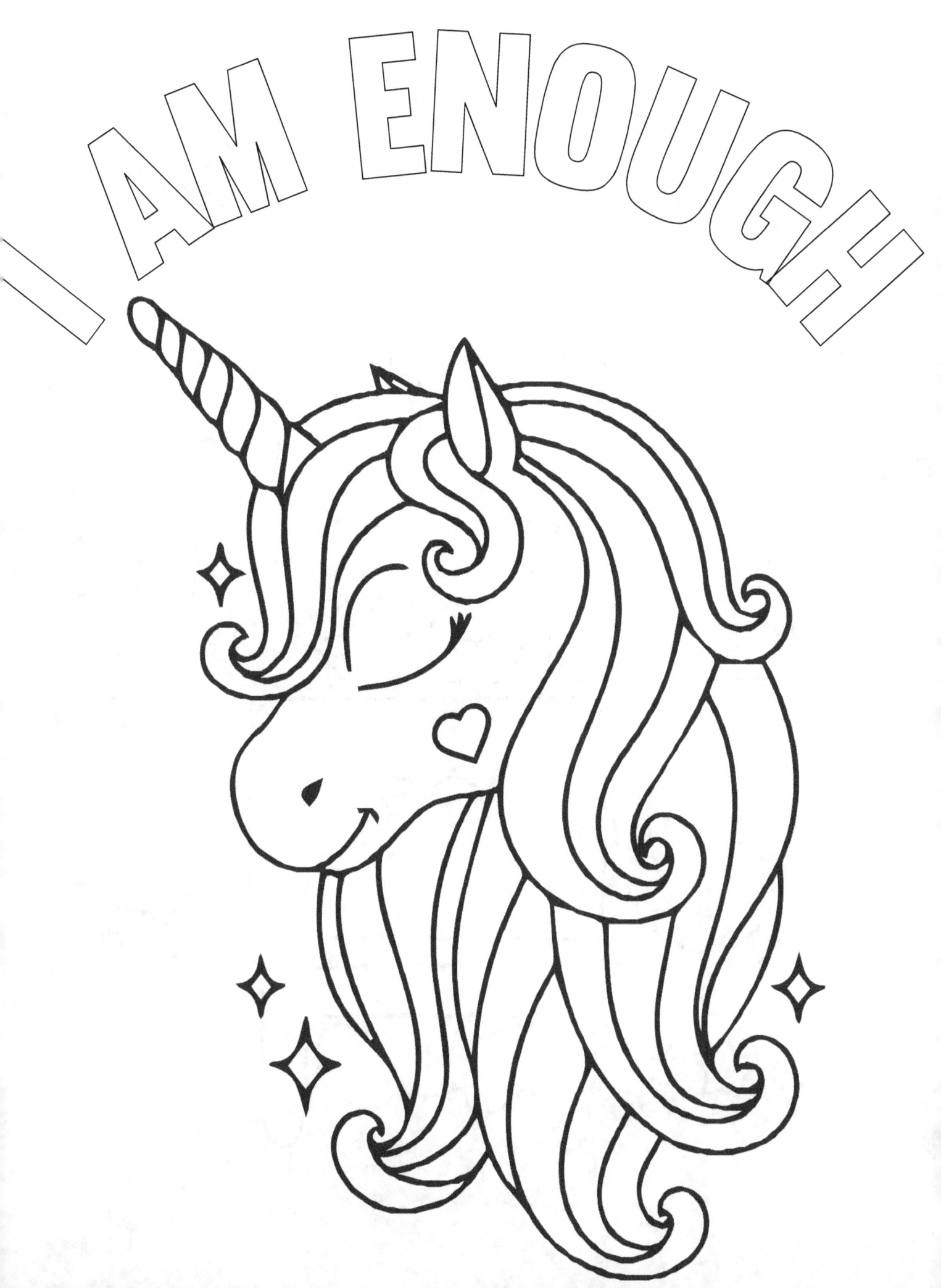

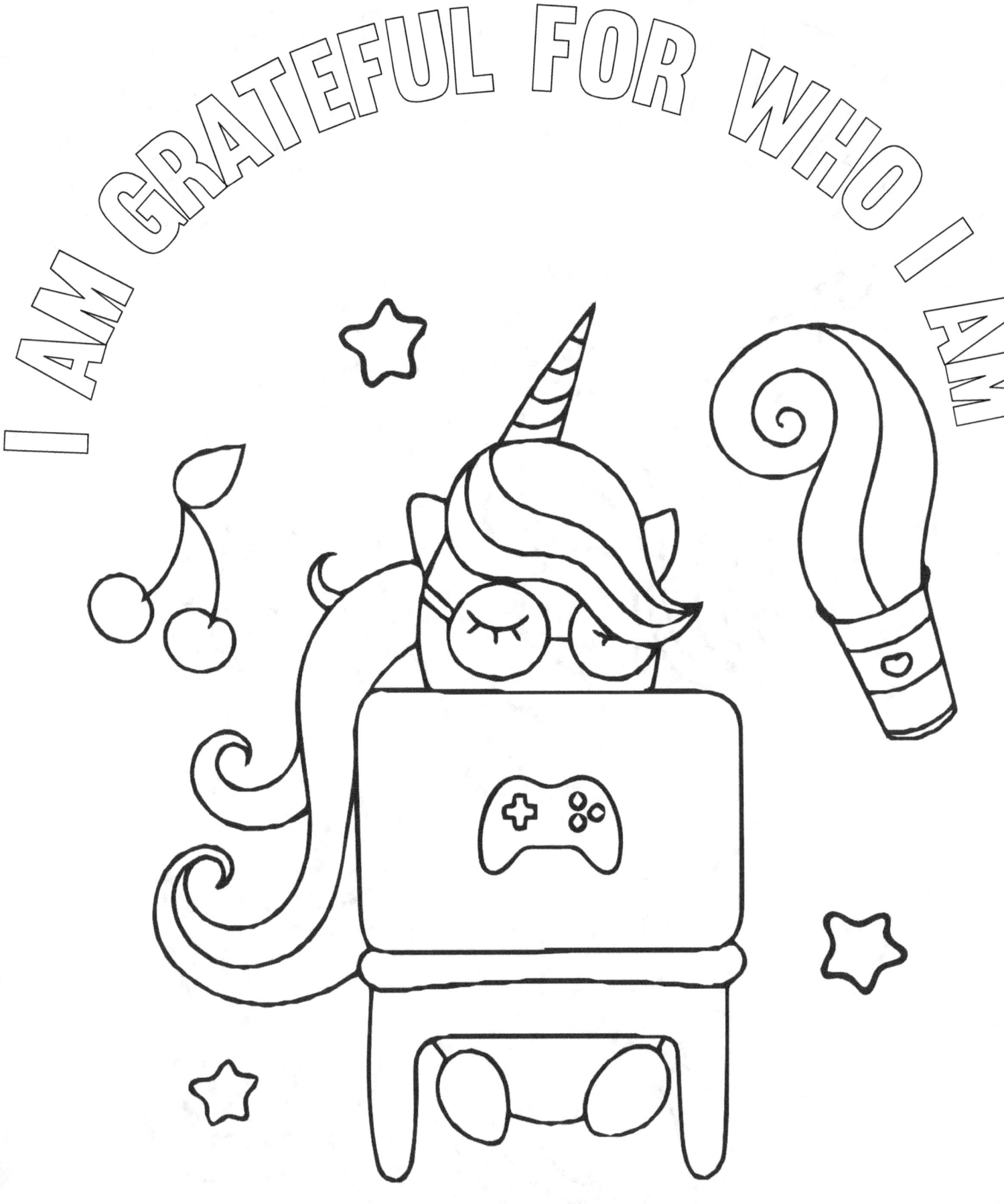

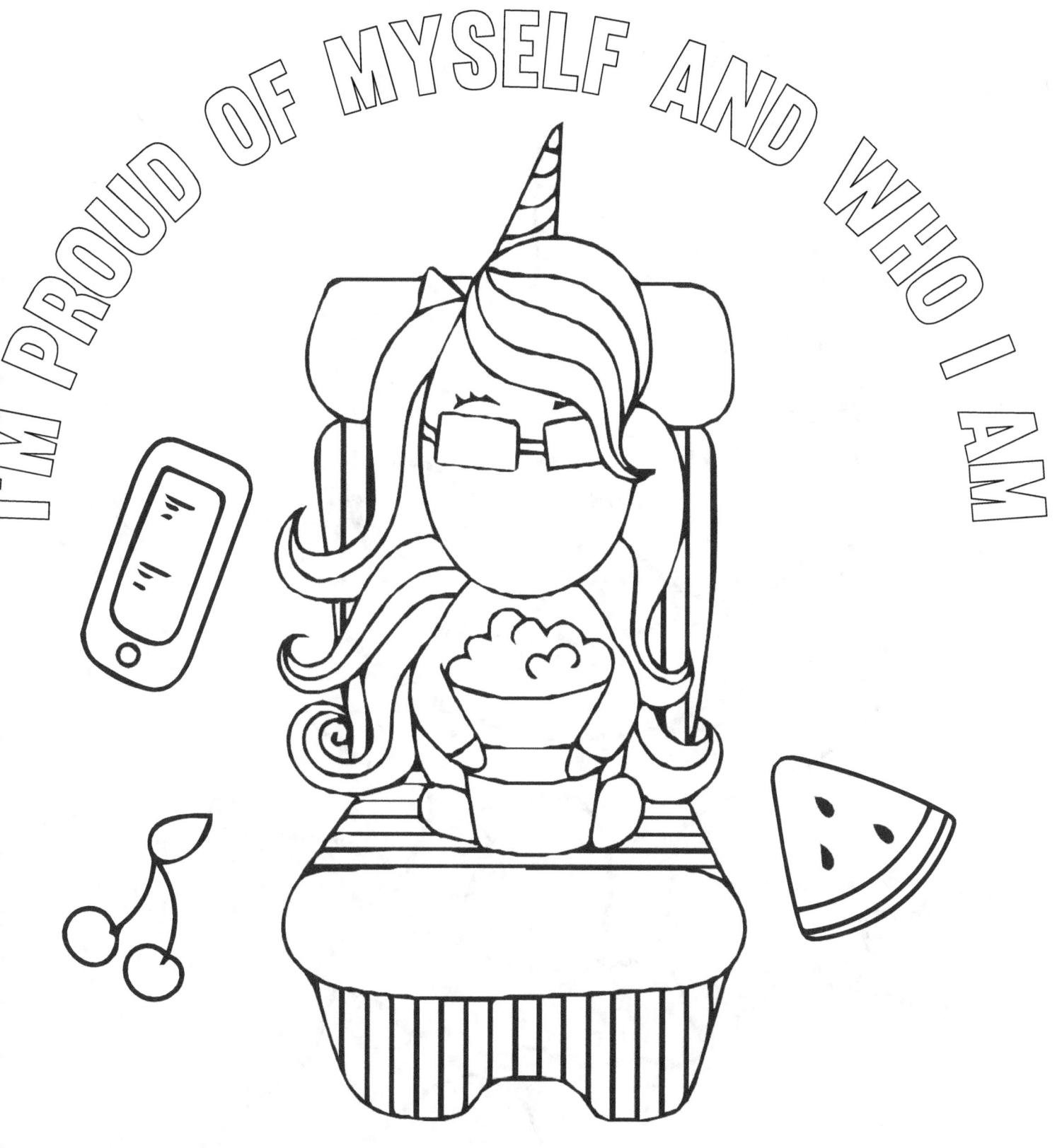

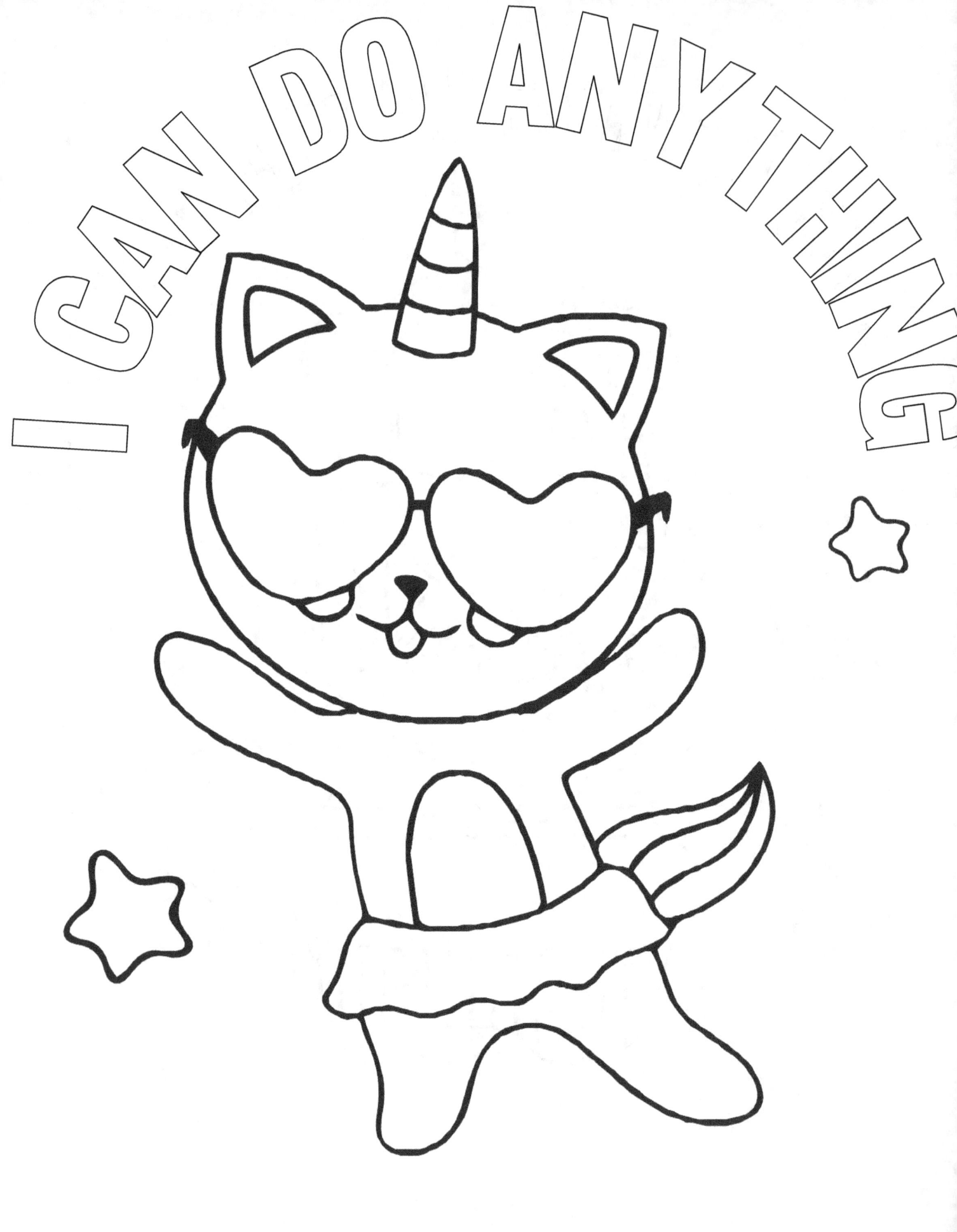

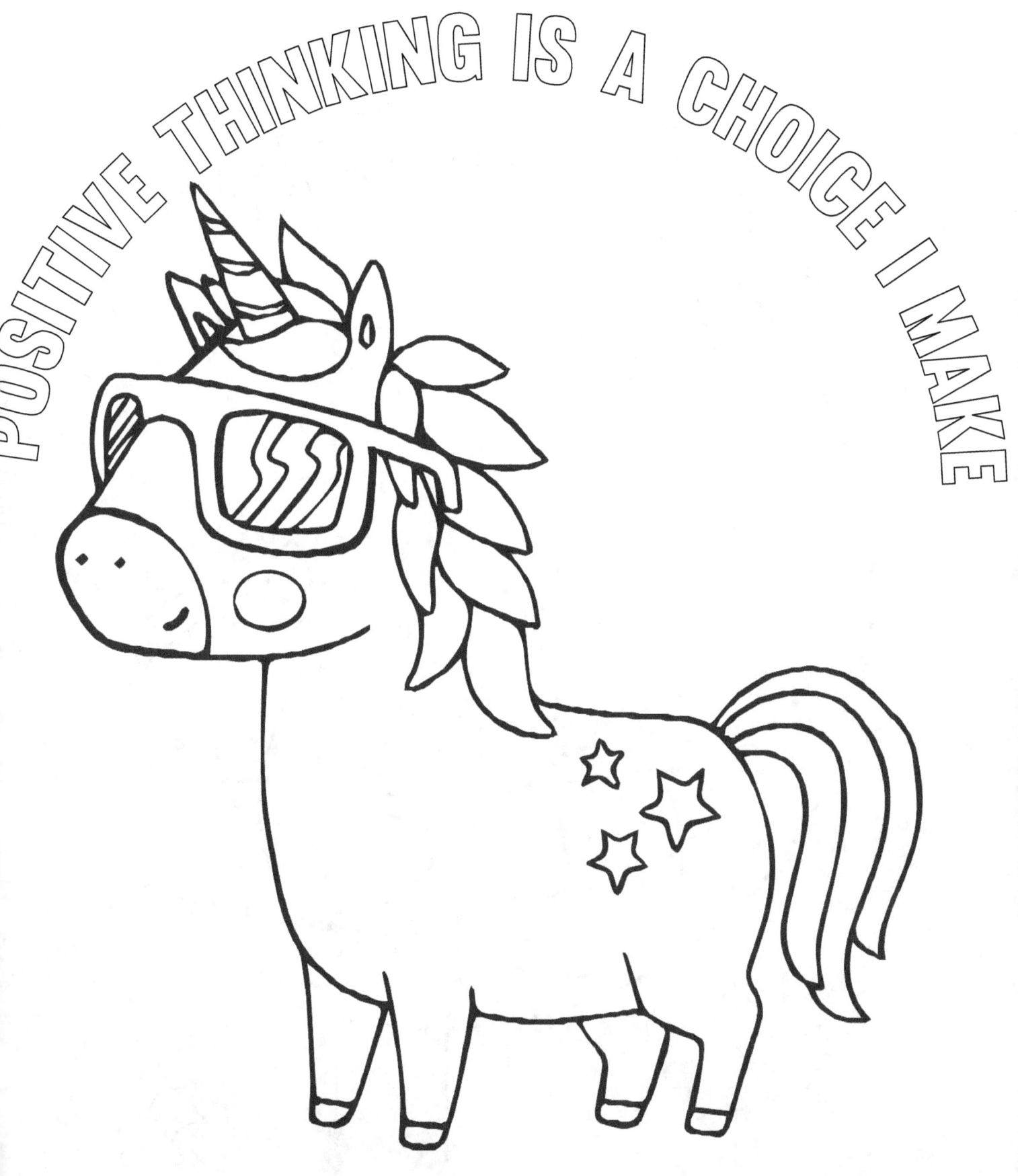

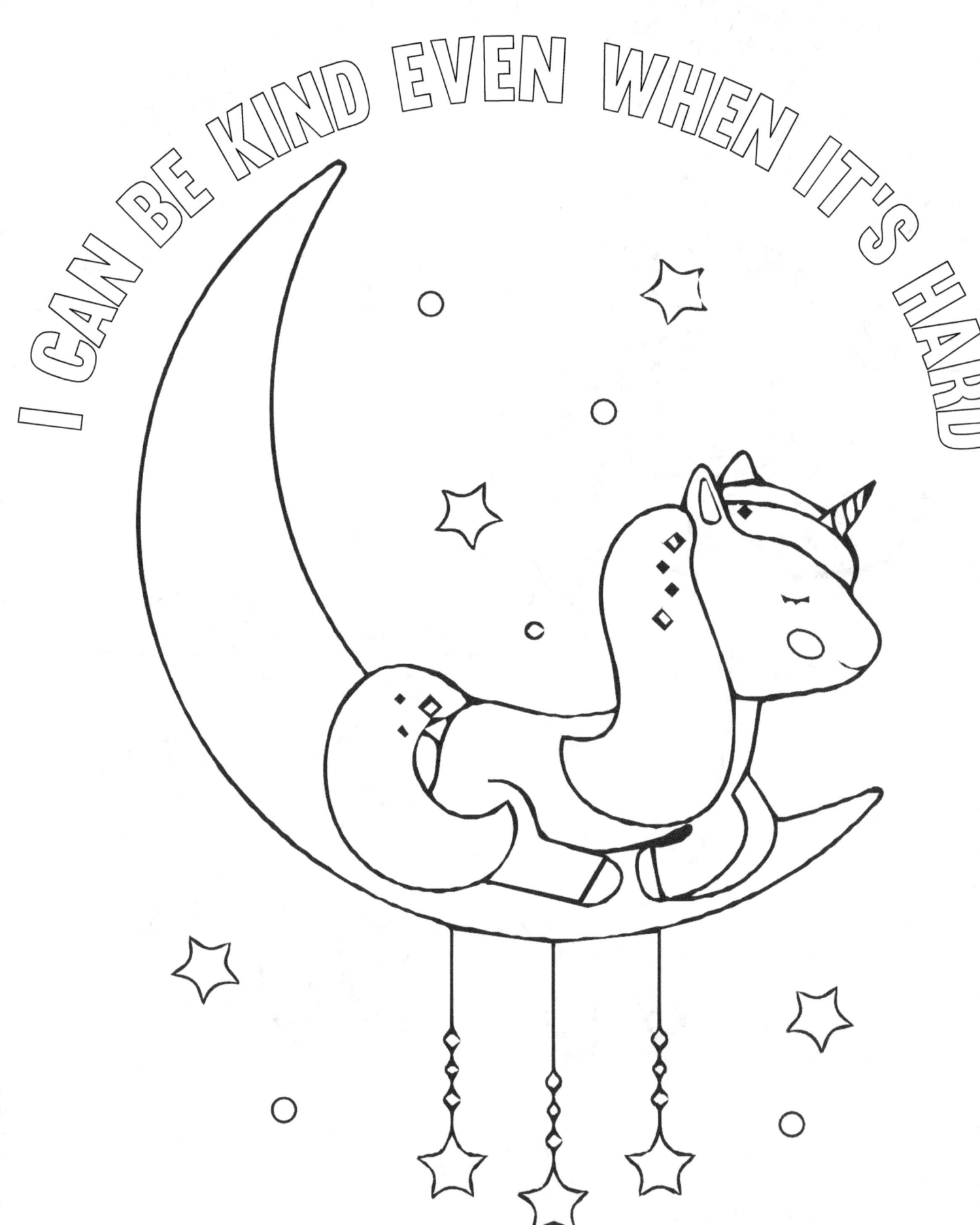

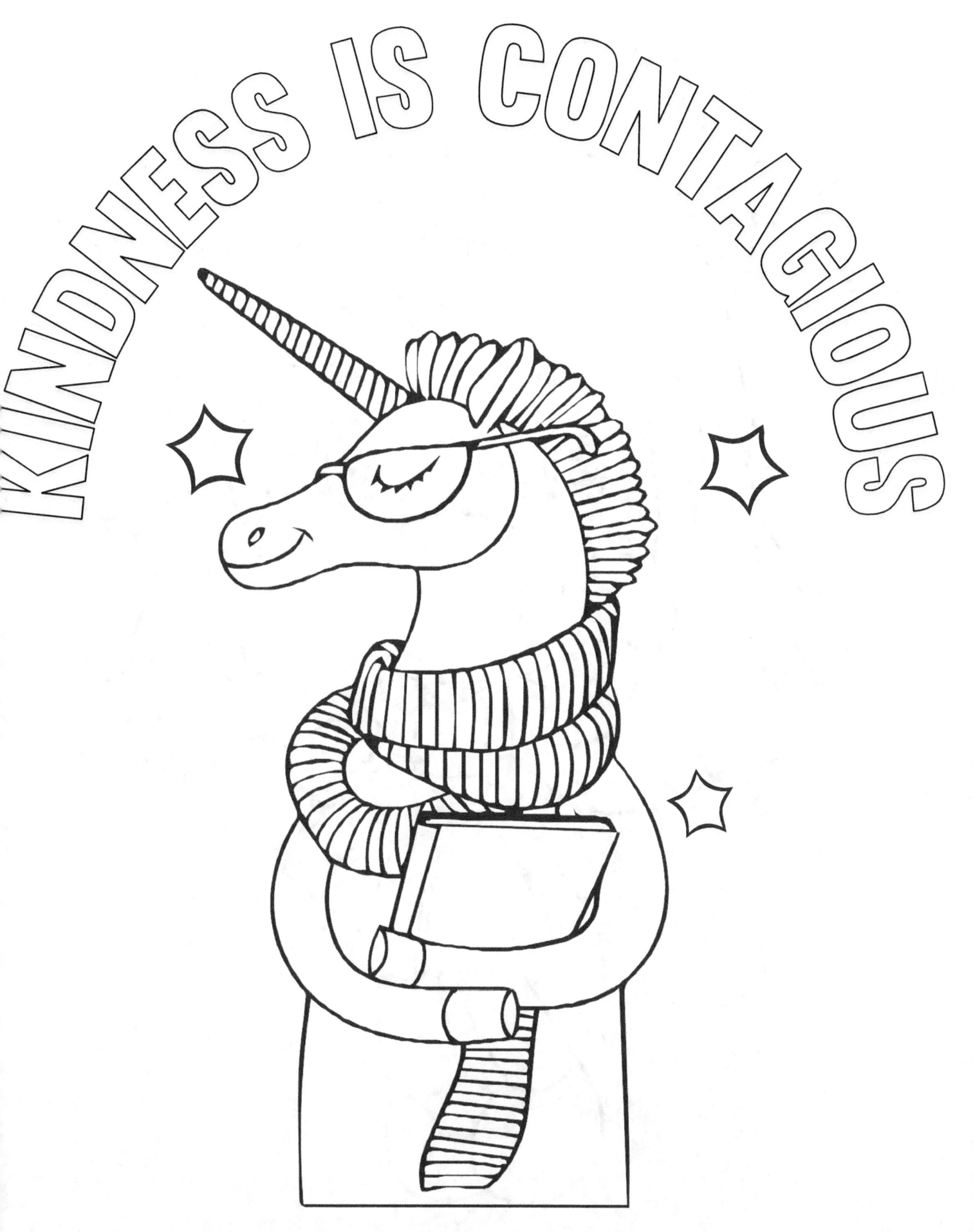

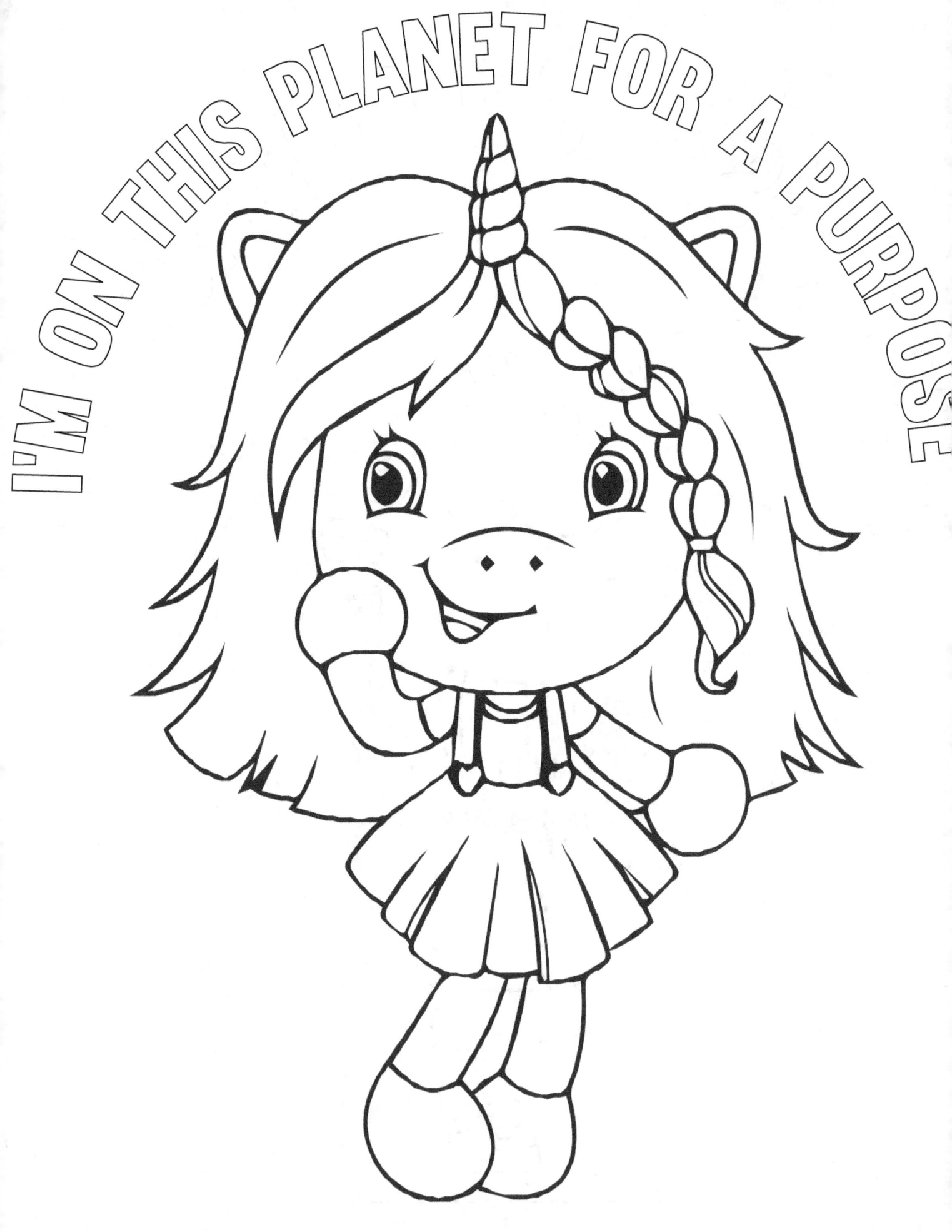

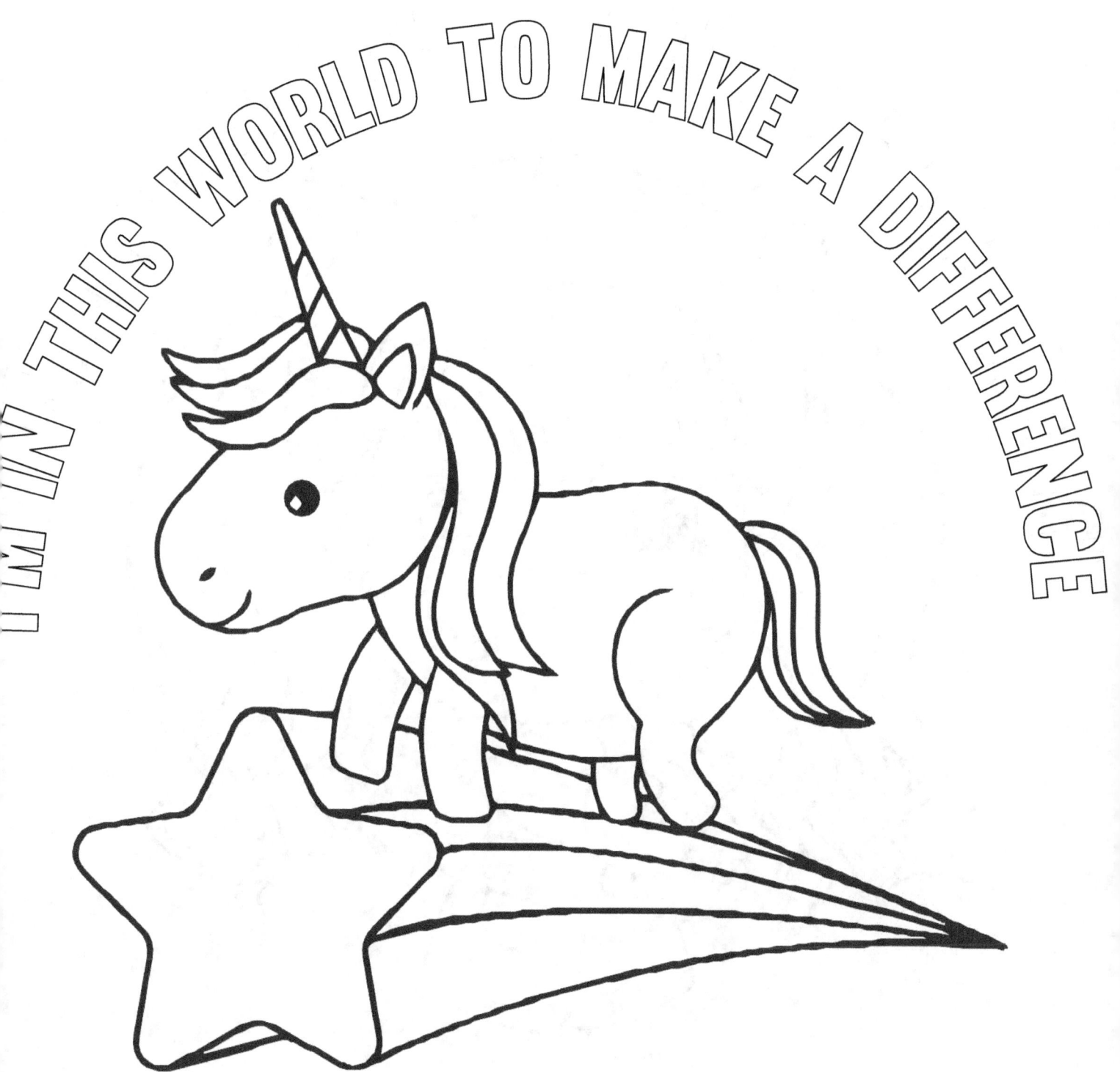

I'M IN IN THIS WORLD TO MAKE A DIFFERENCE

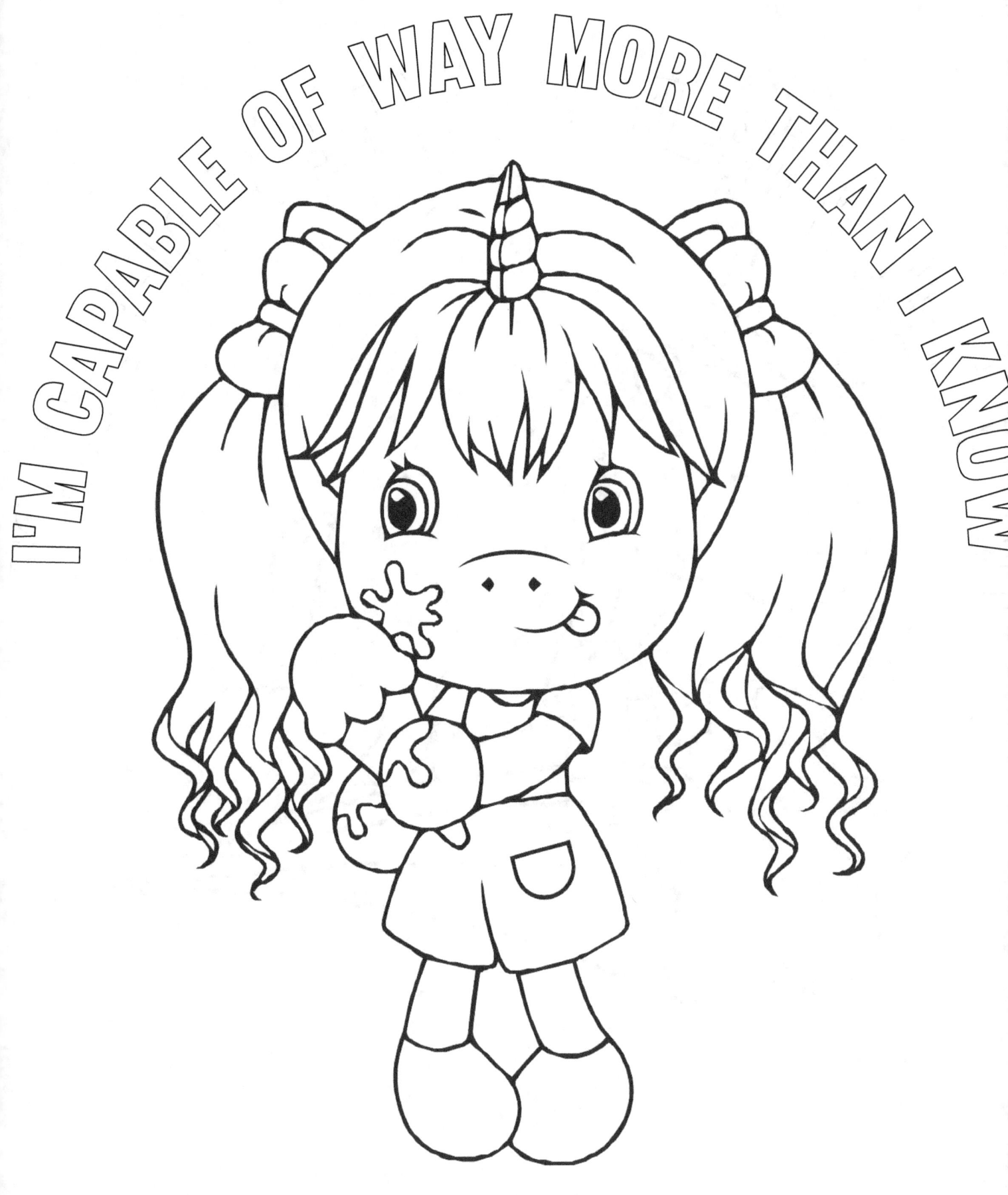

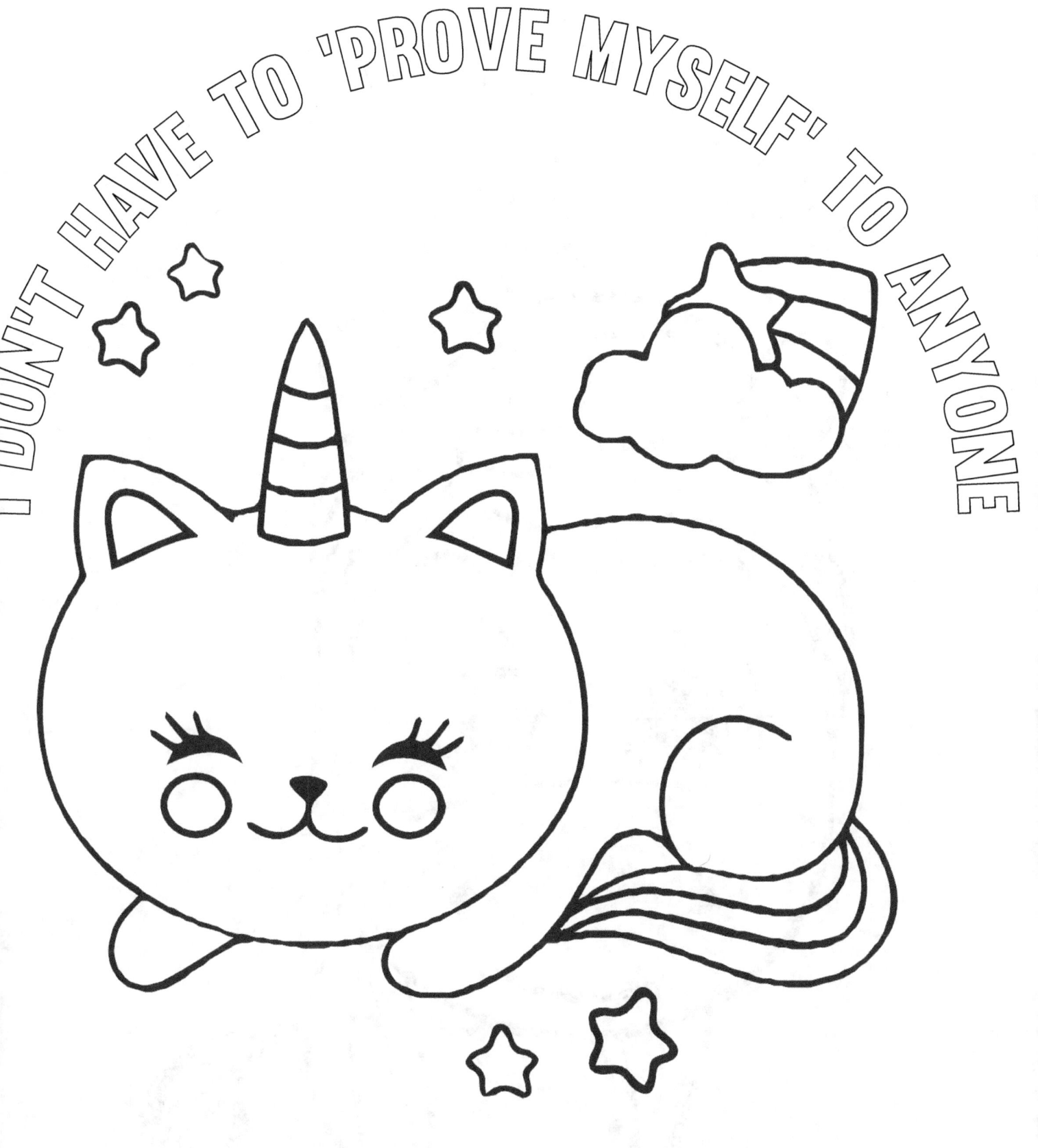

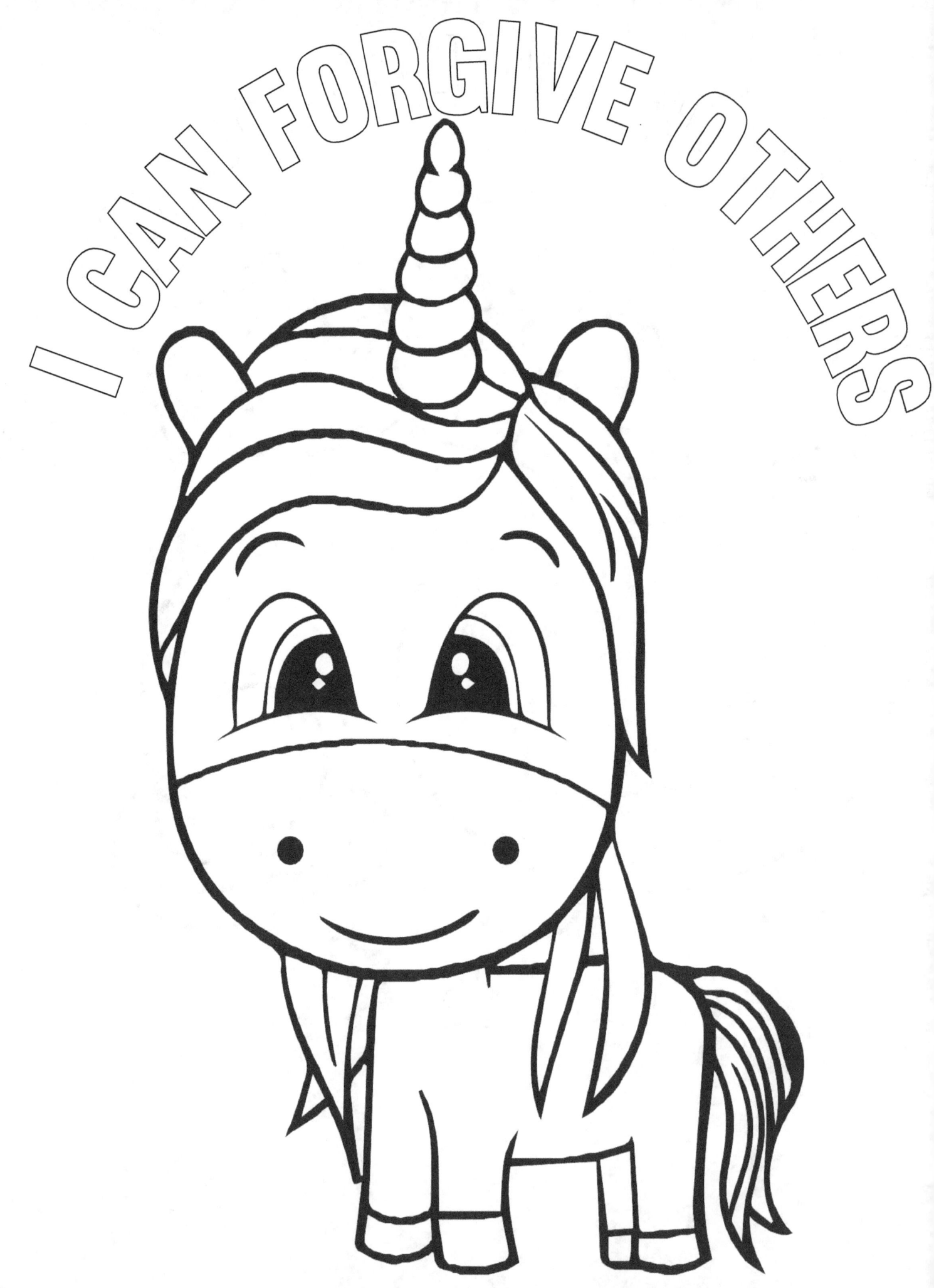

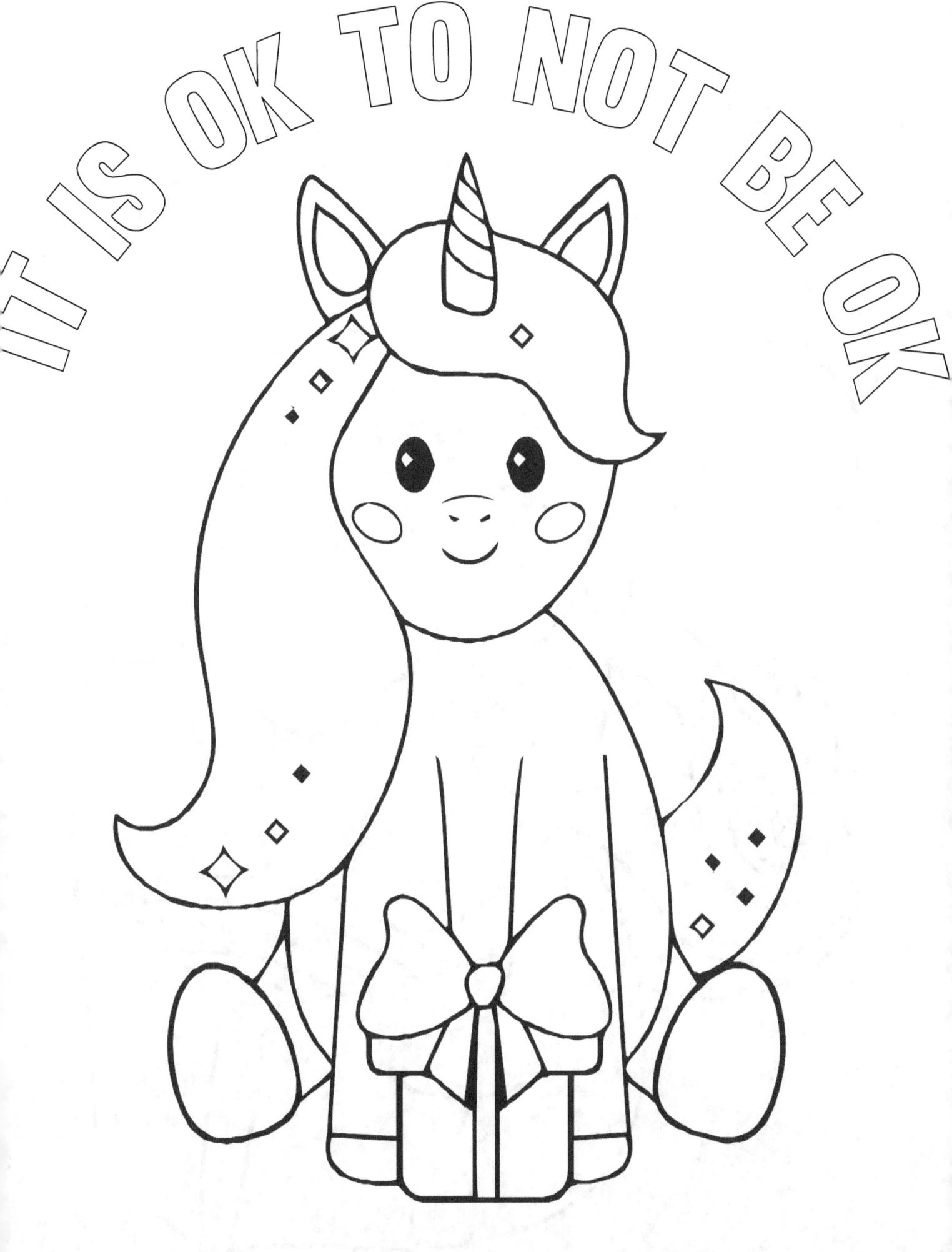

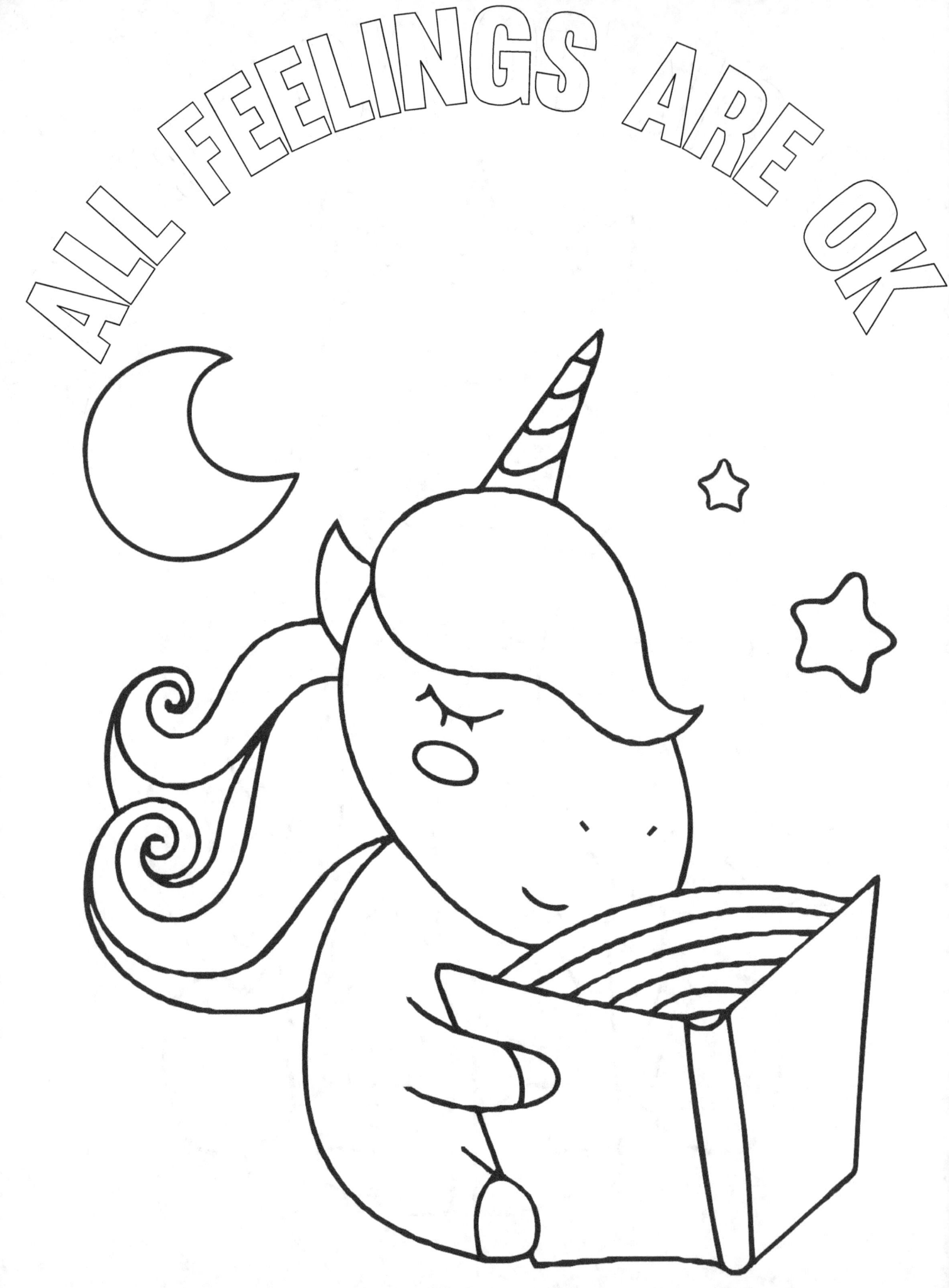

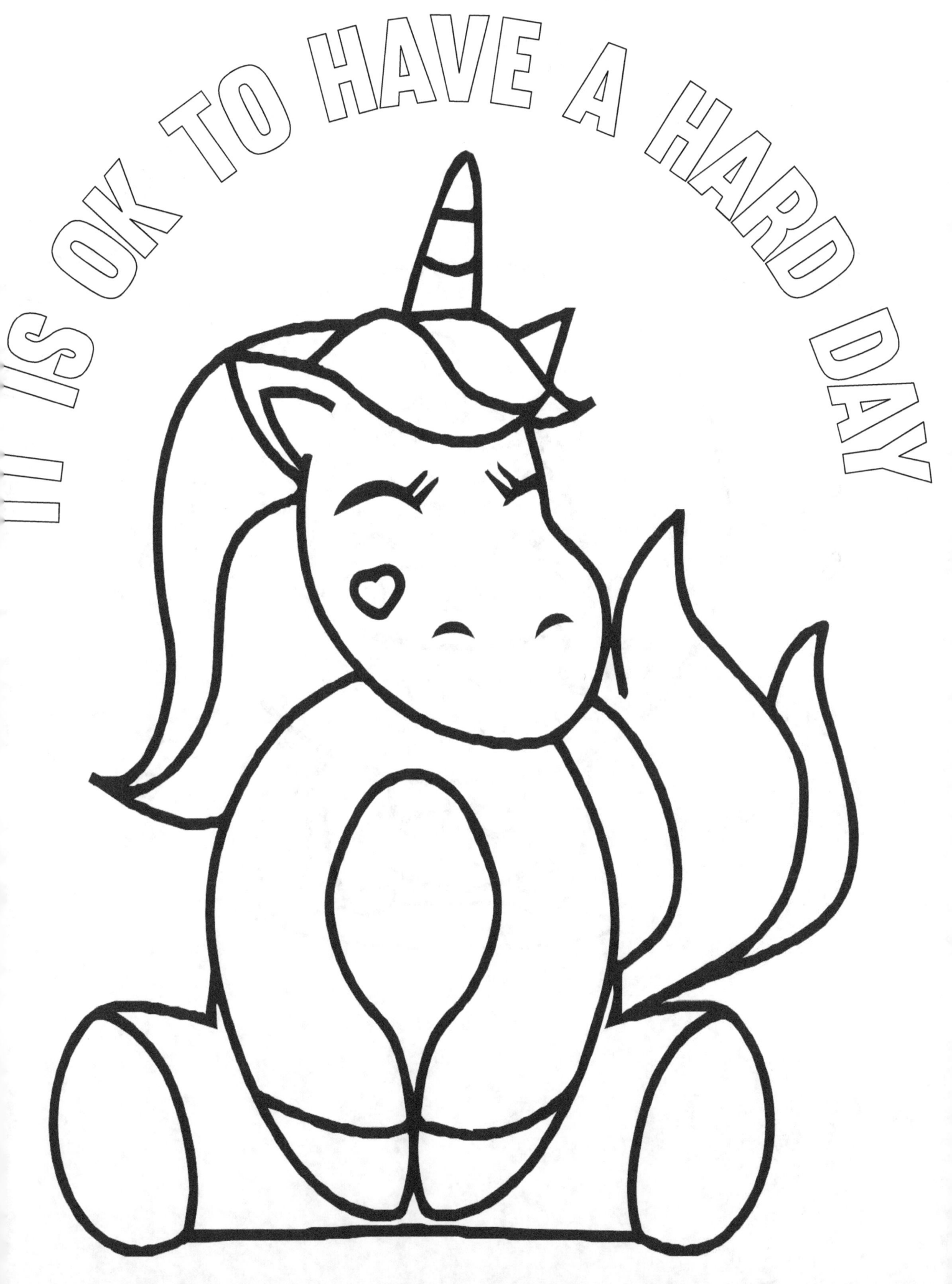

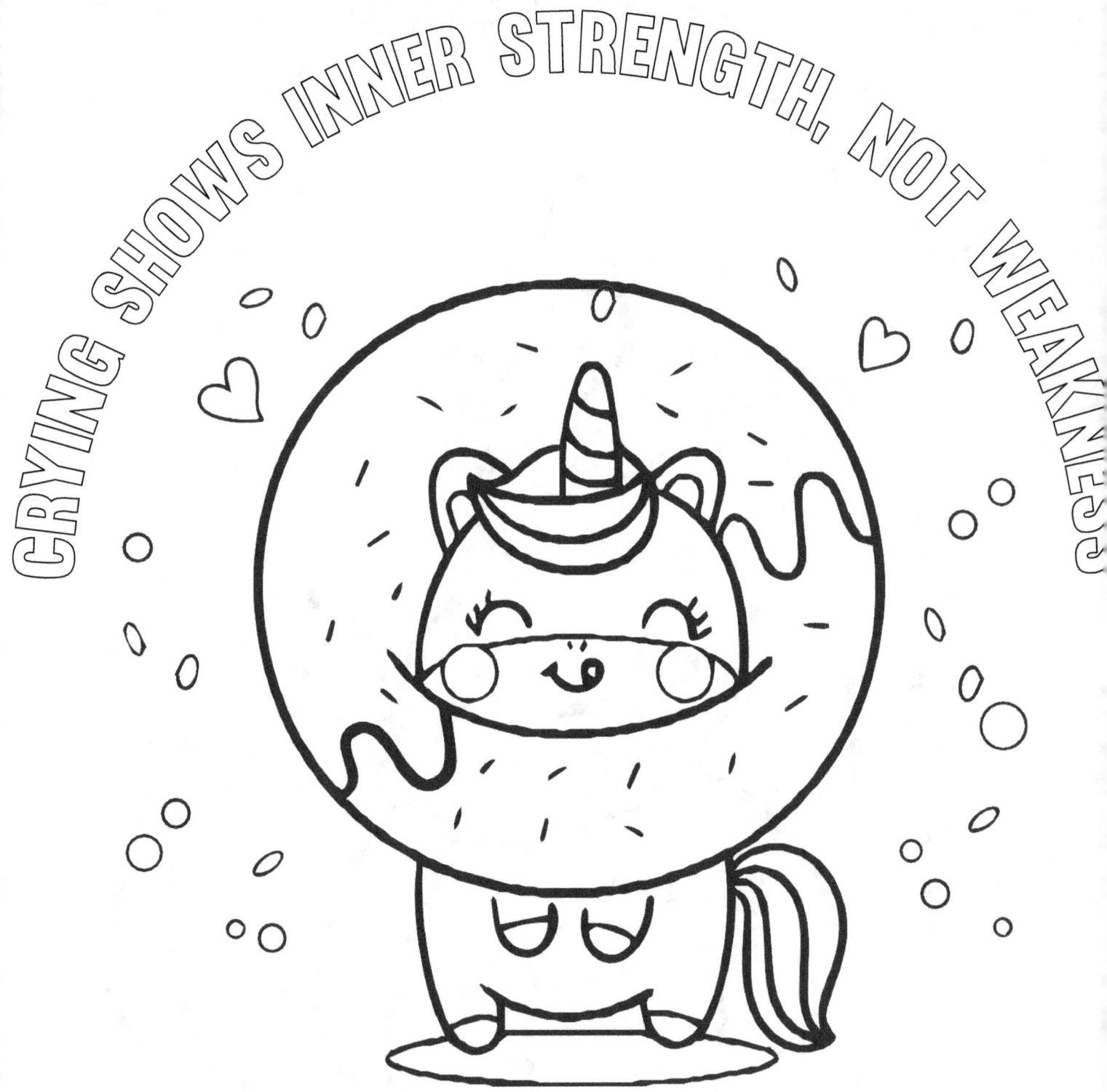

CRYING SHOWS INNER STRENGTH, NOT WEAKNESS

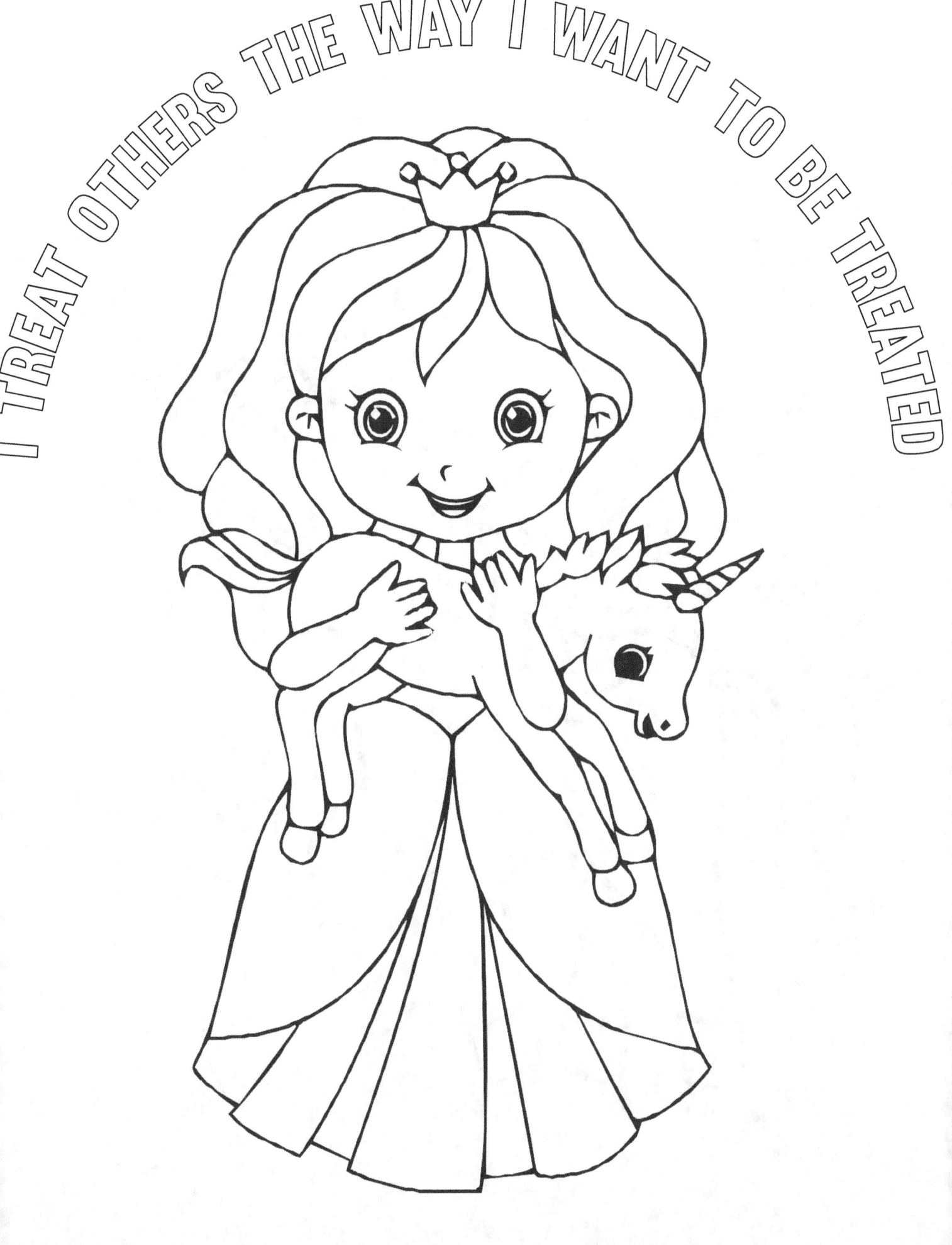

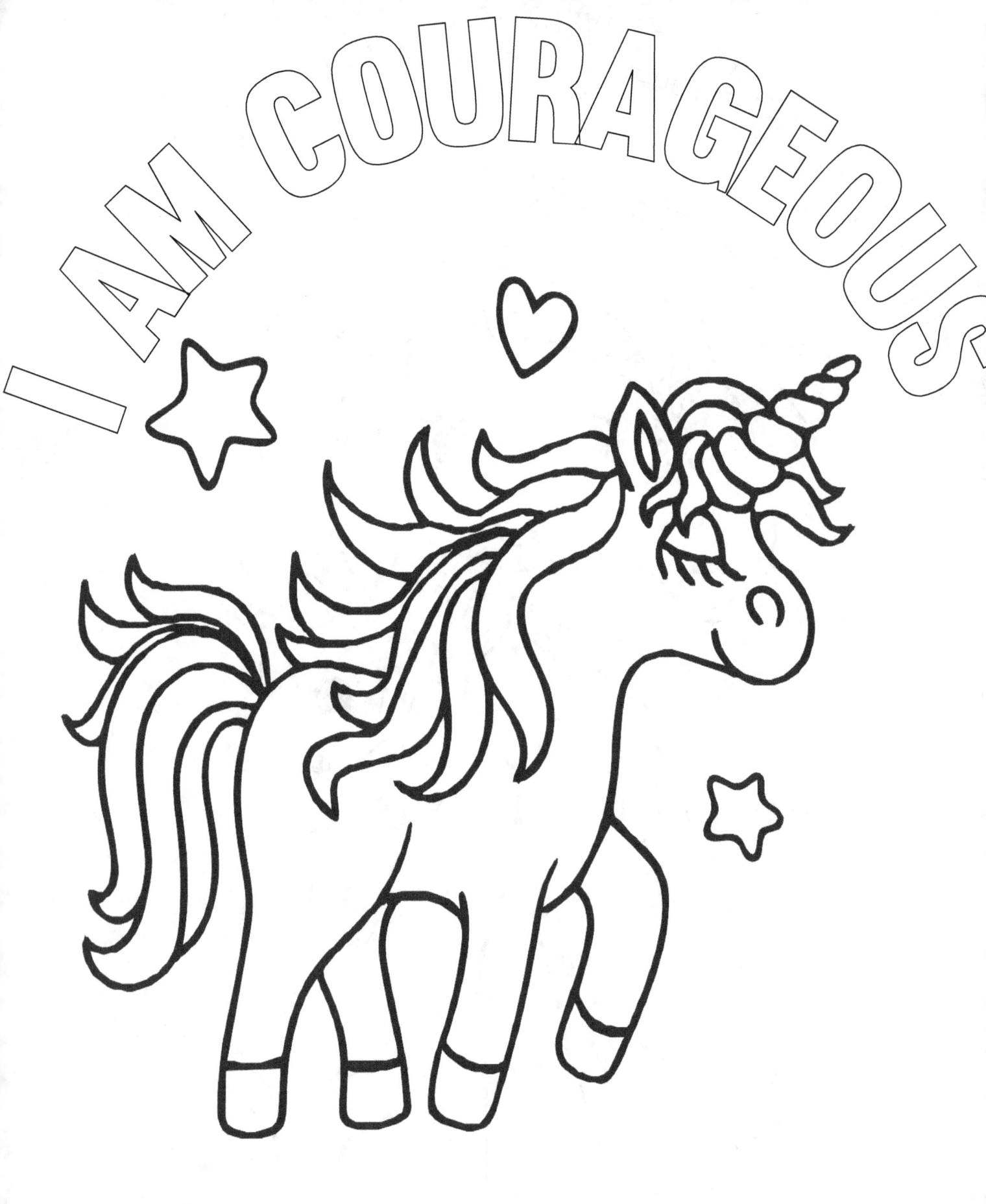

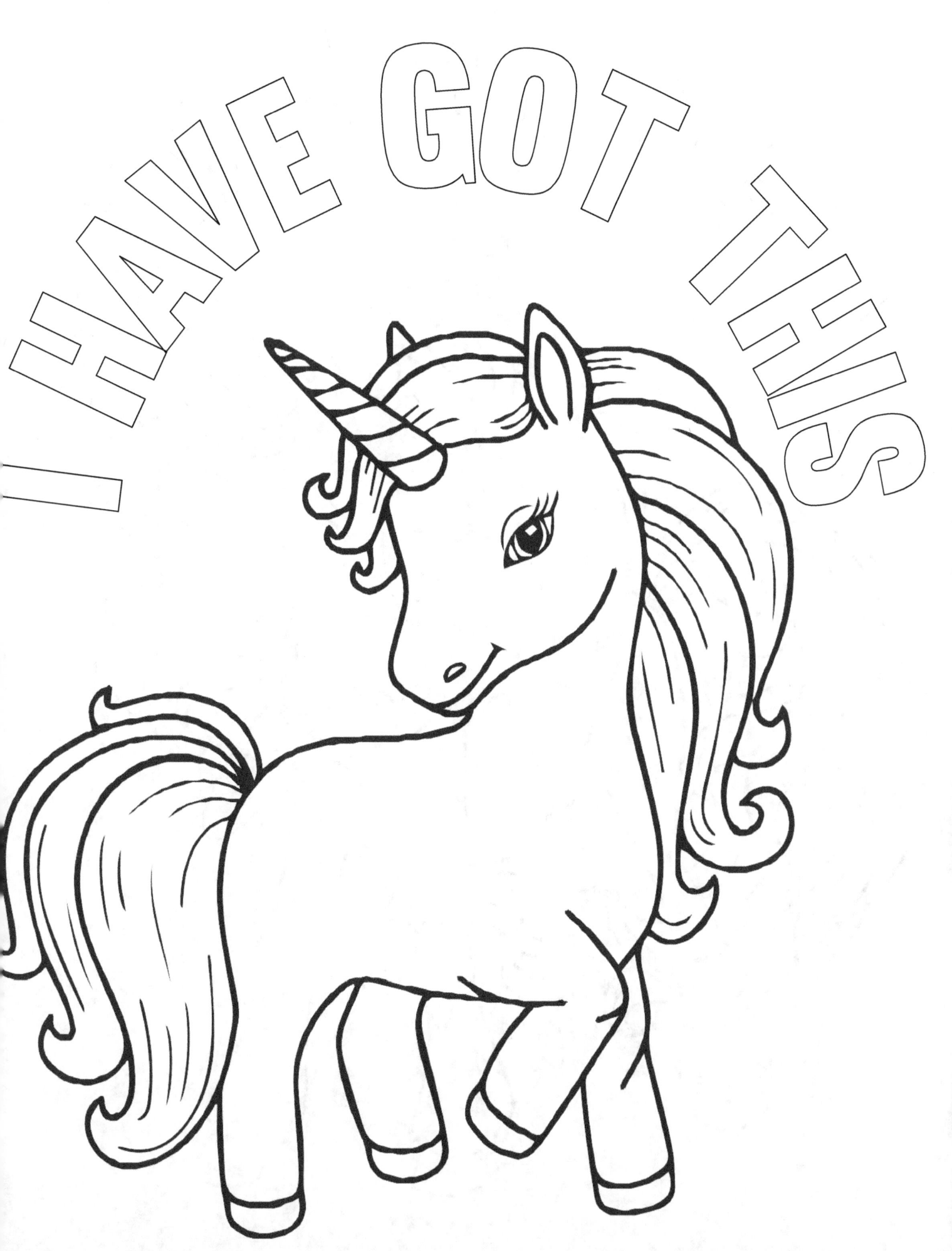

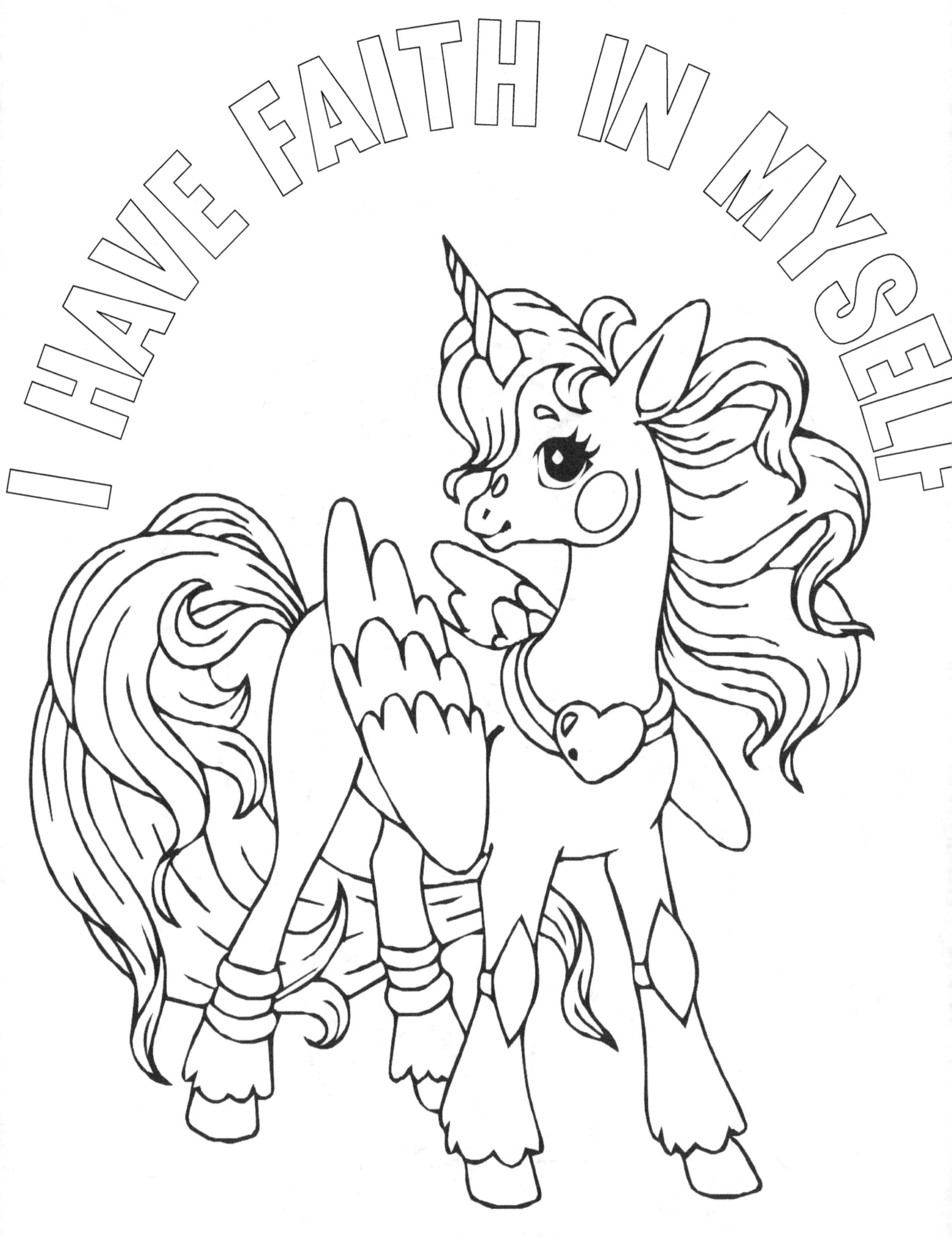

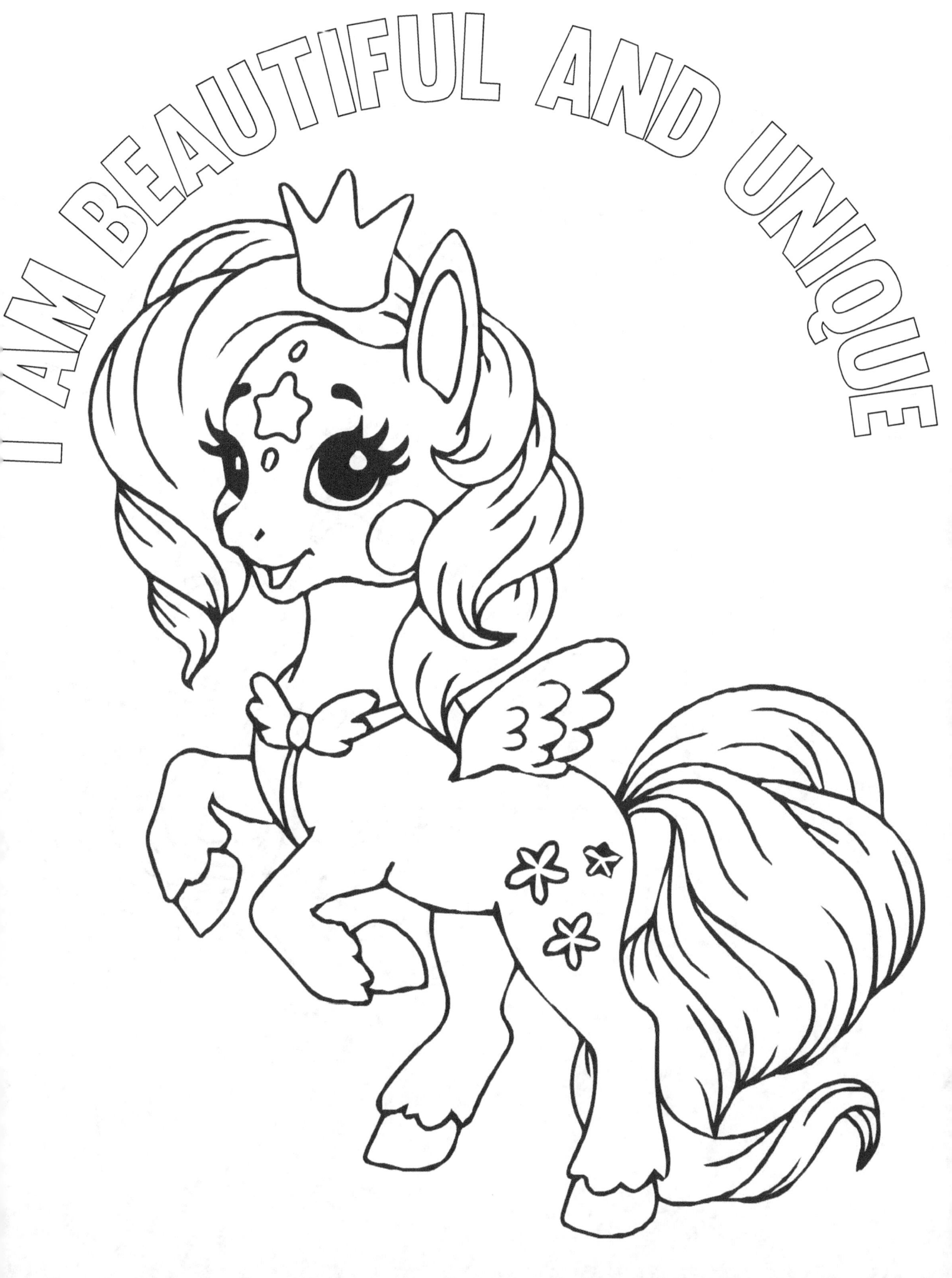

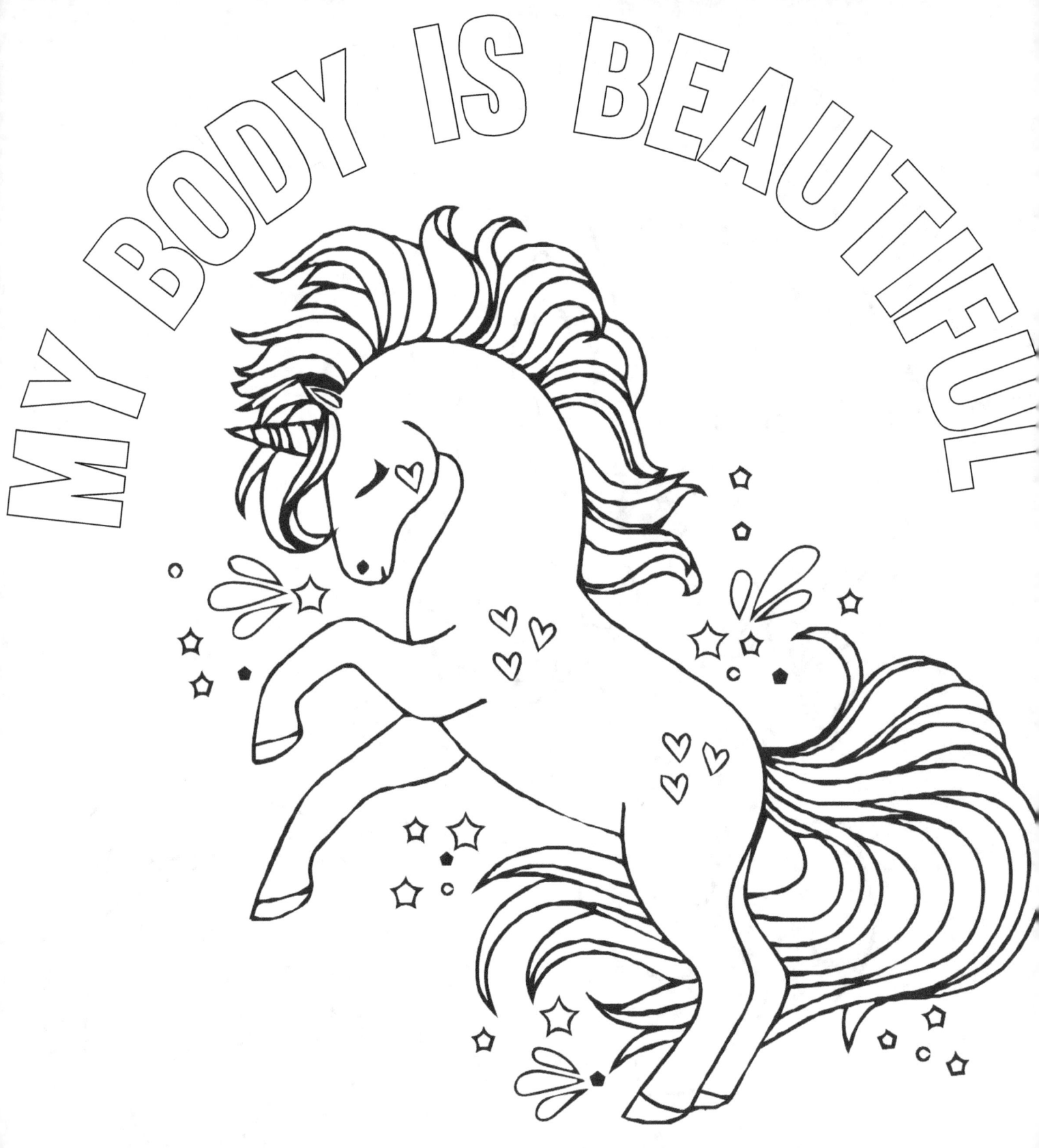

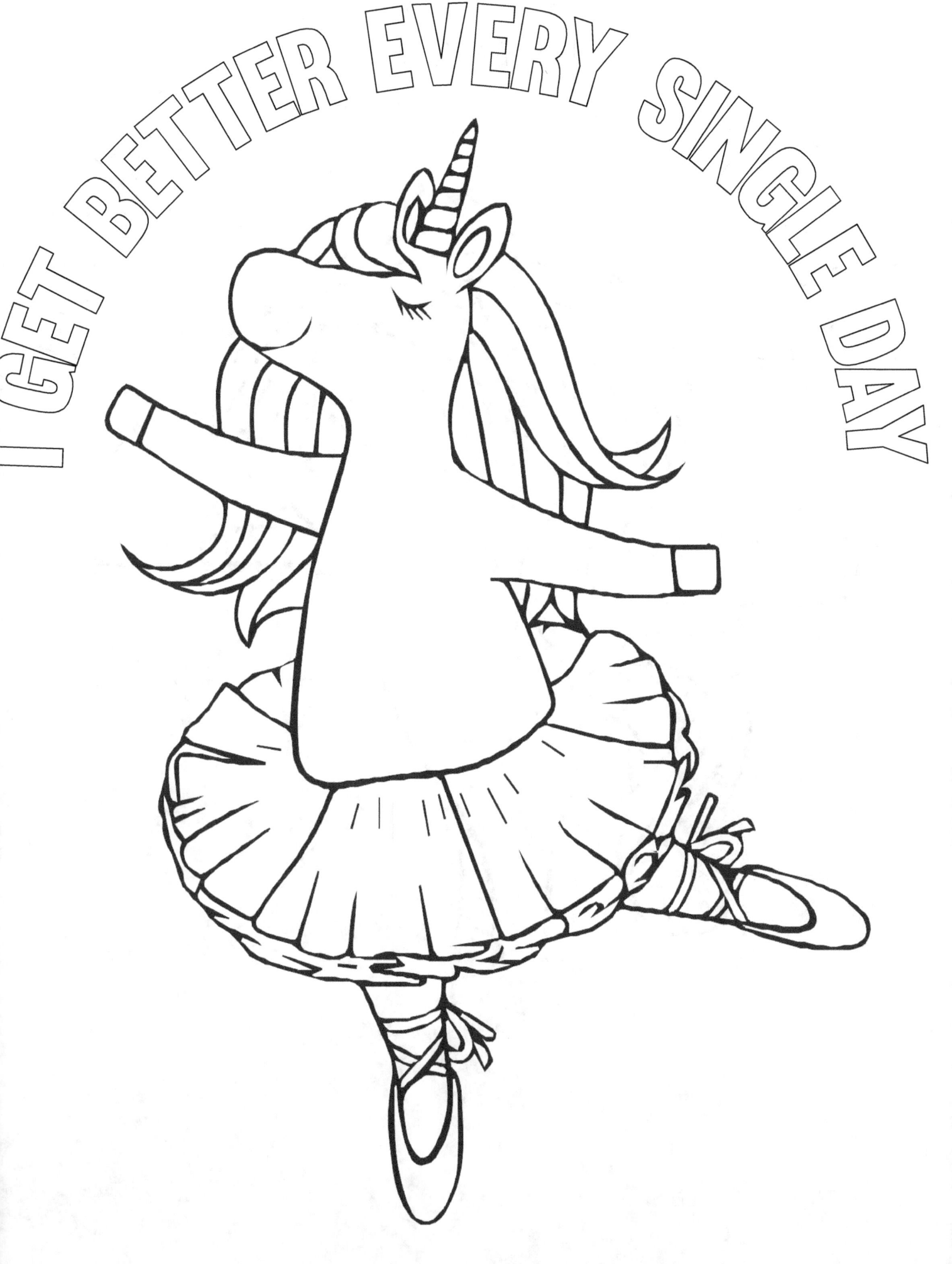

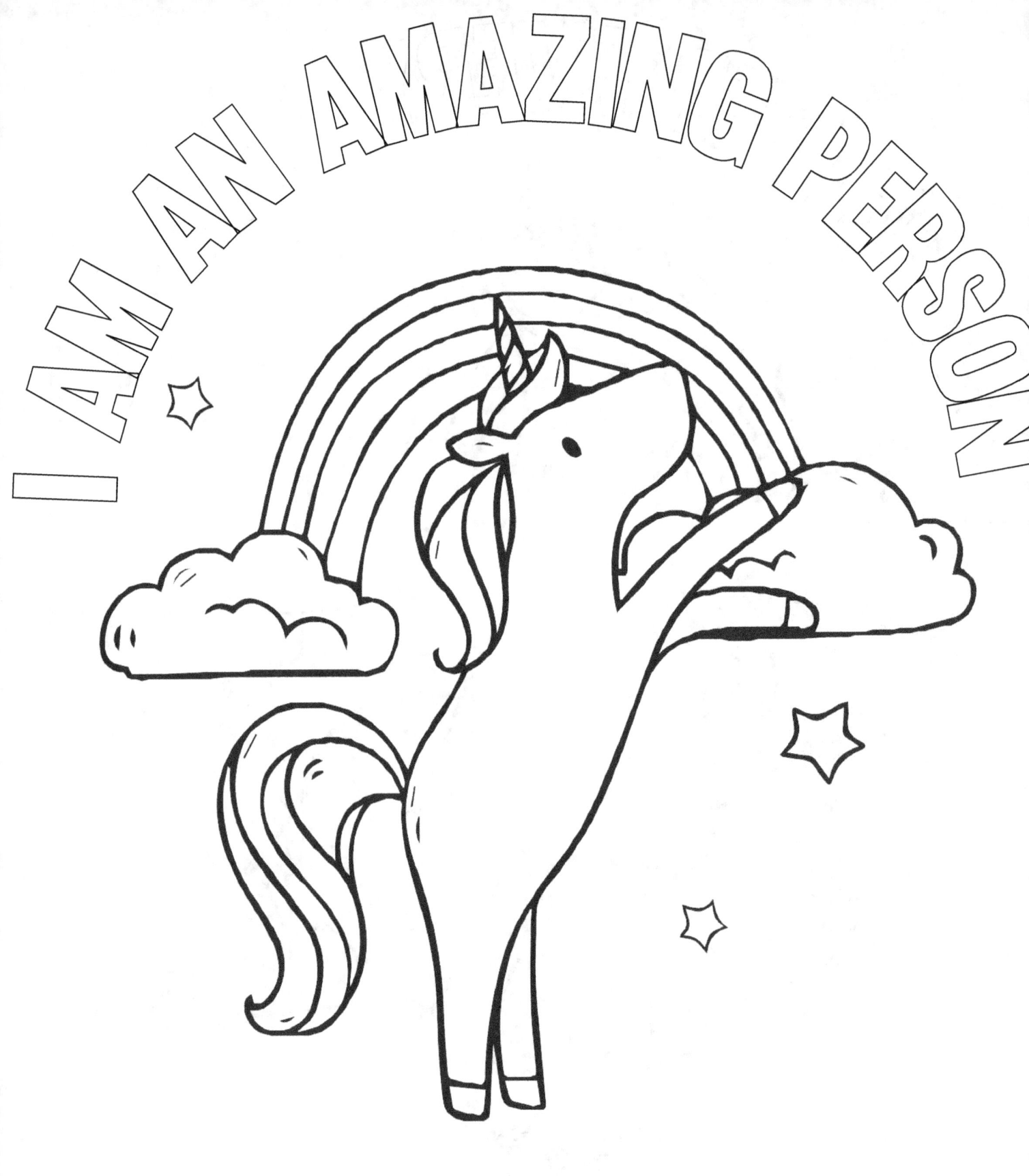

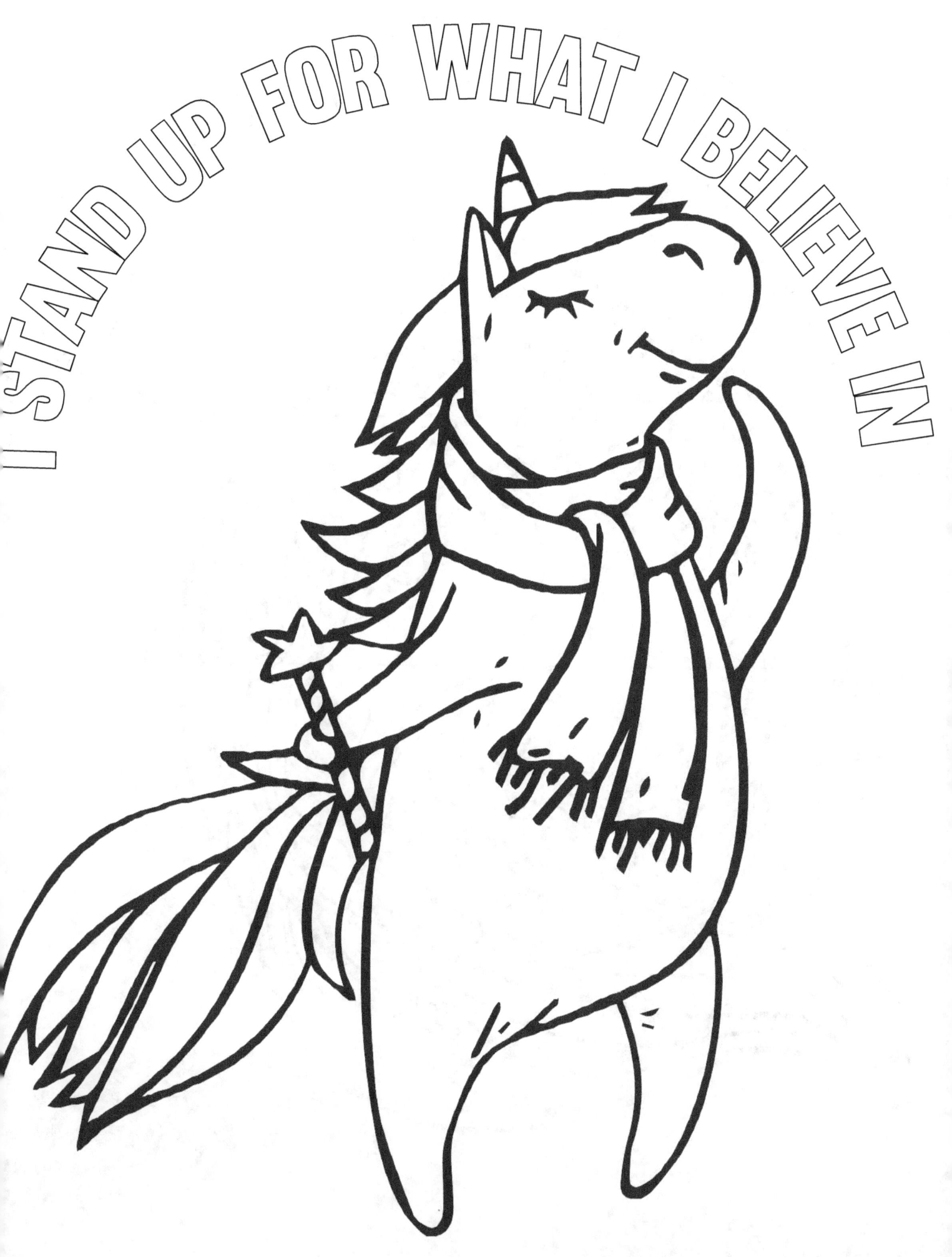

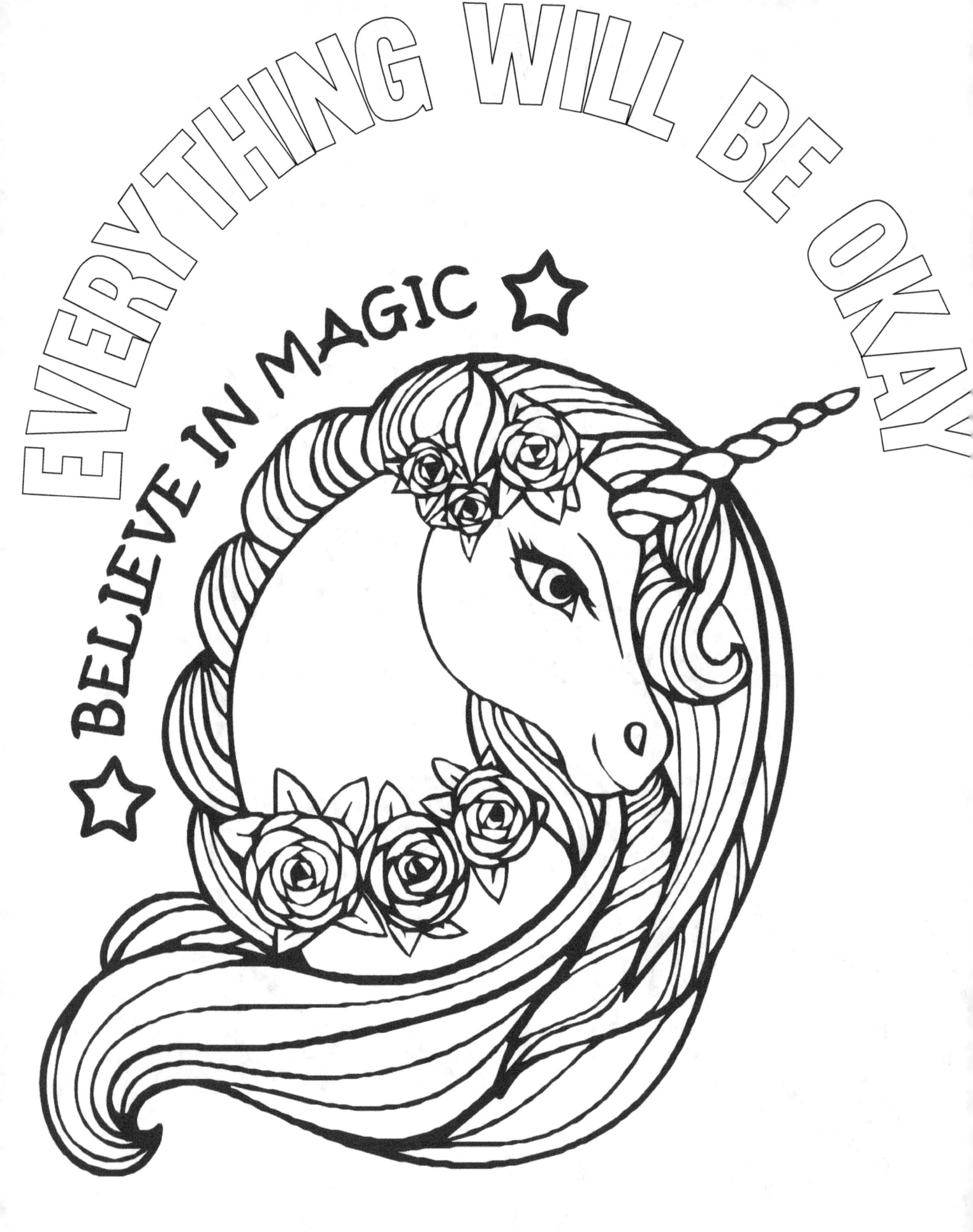

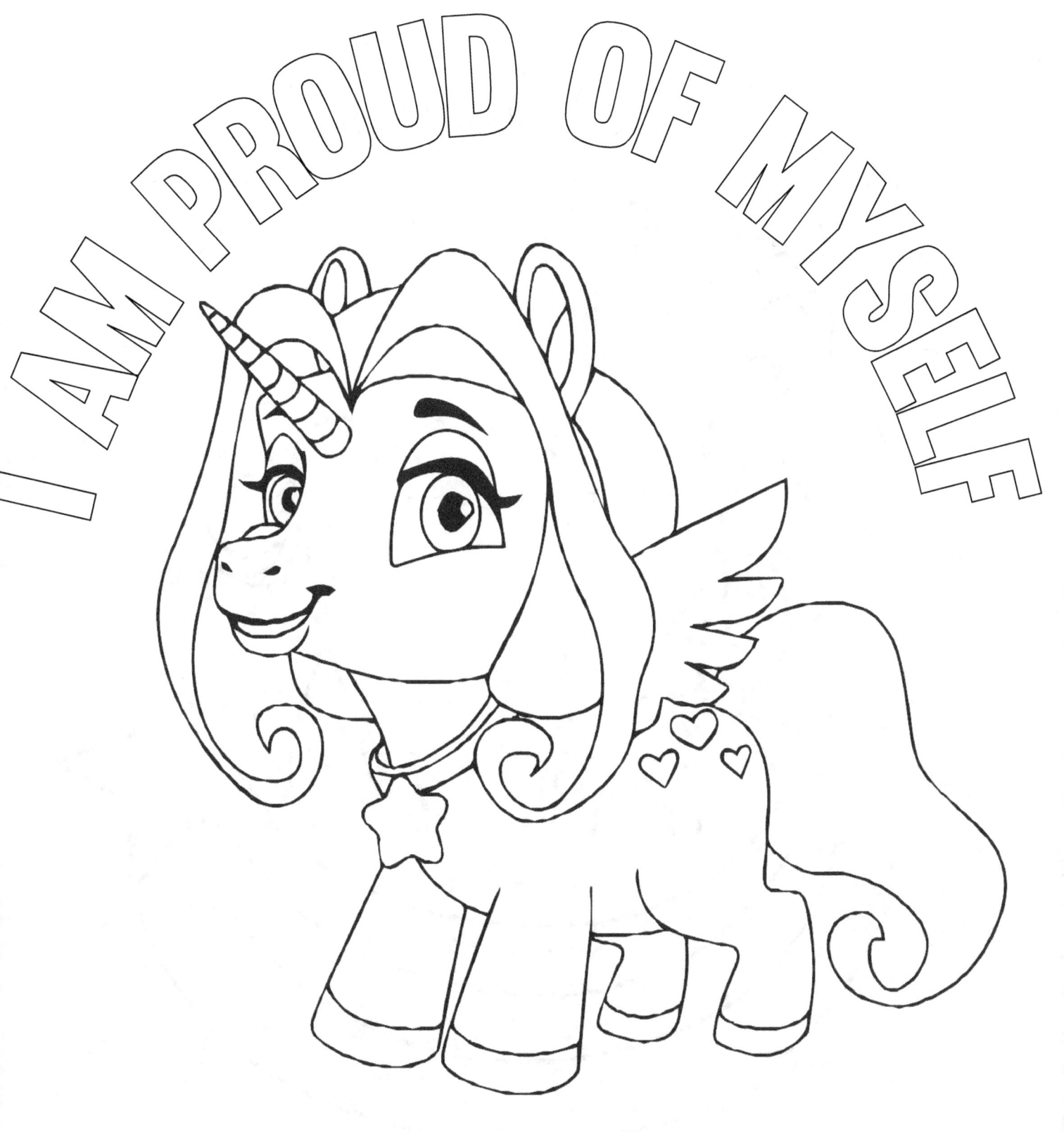

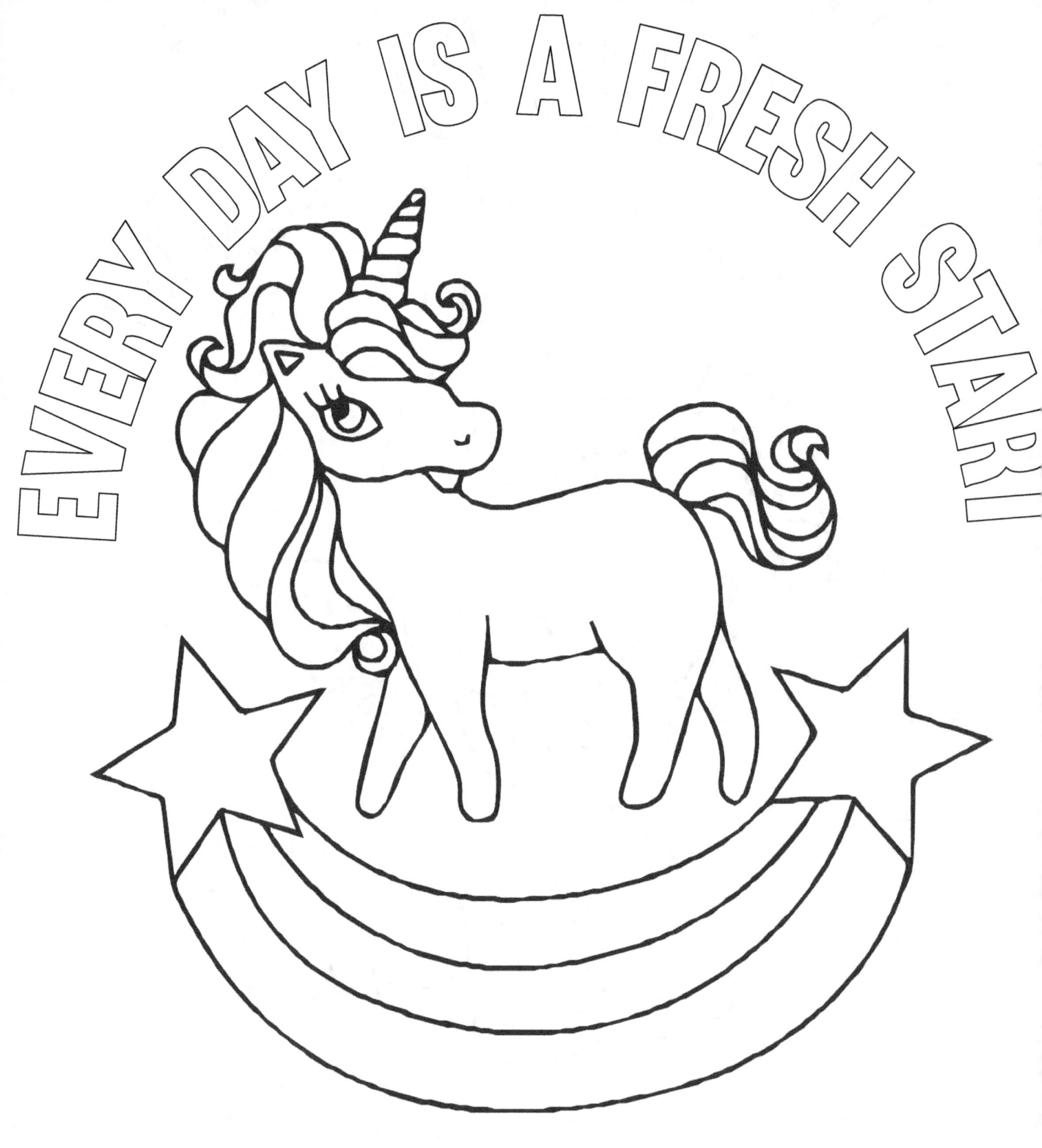

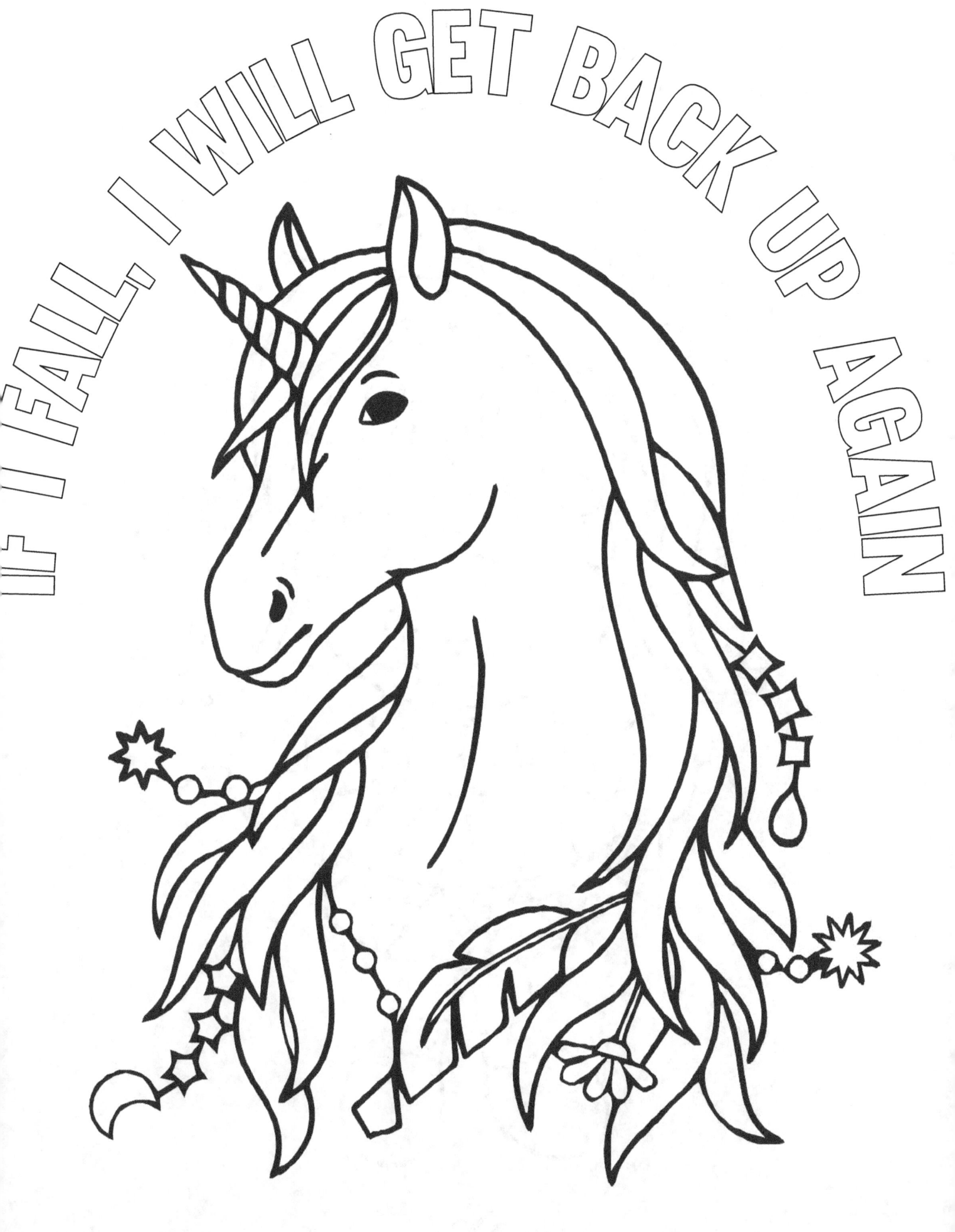

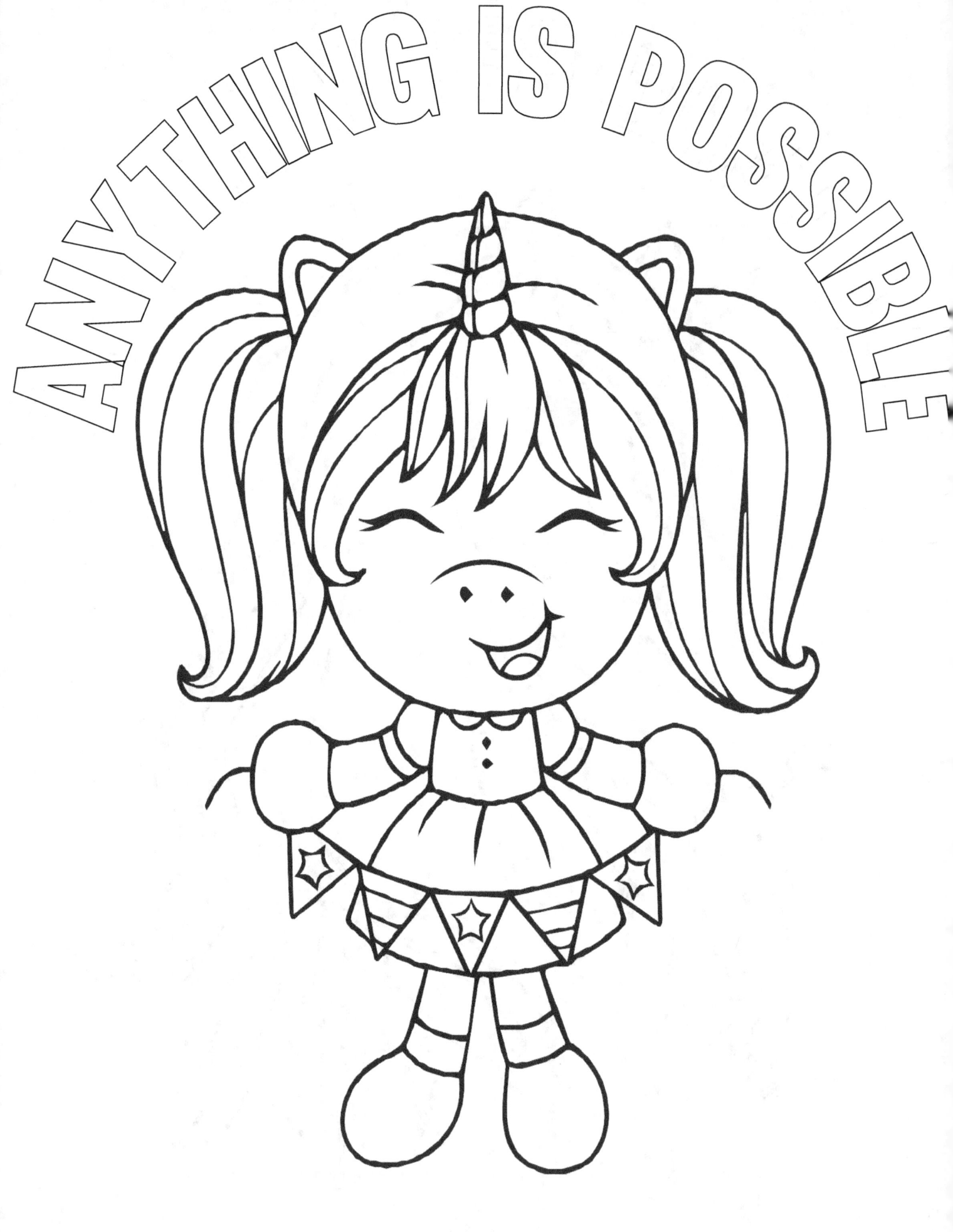

I AM AN ORIGINAL

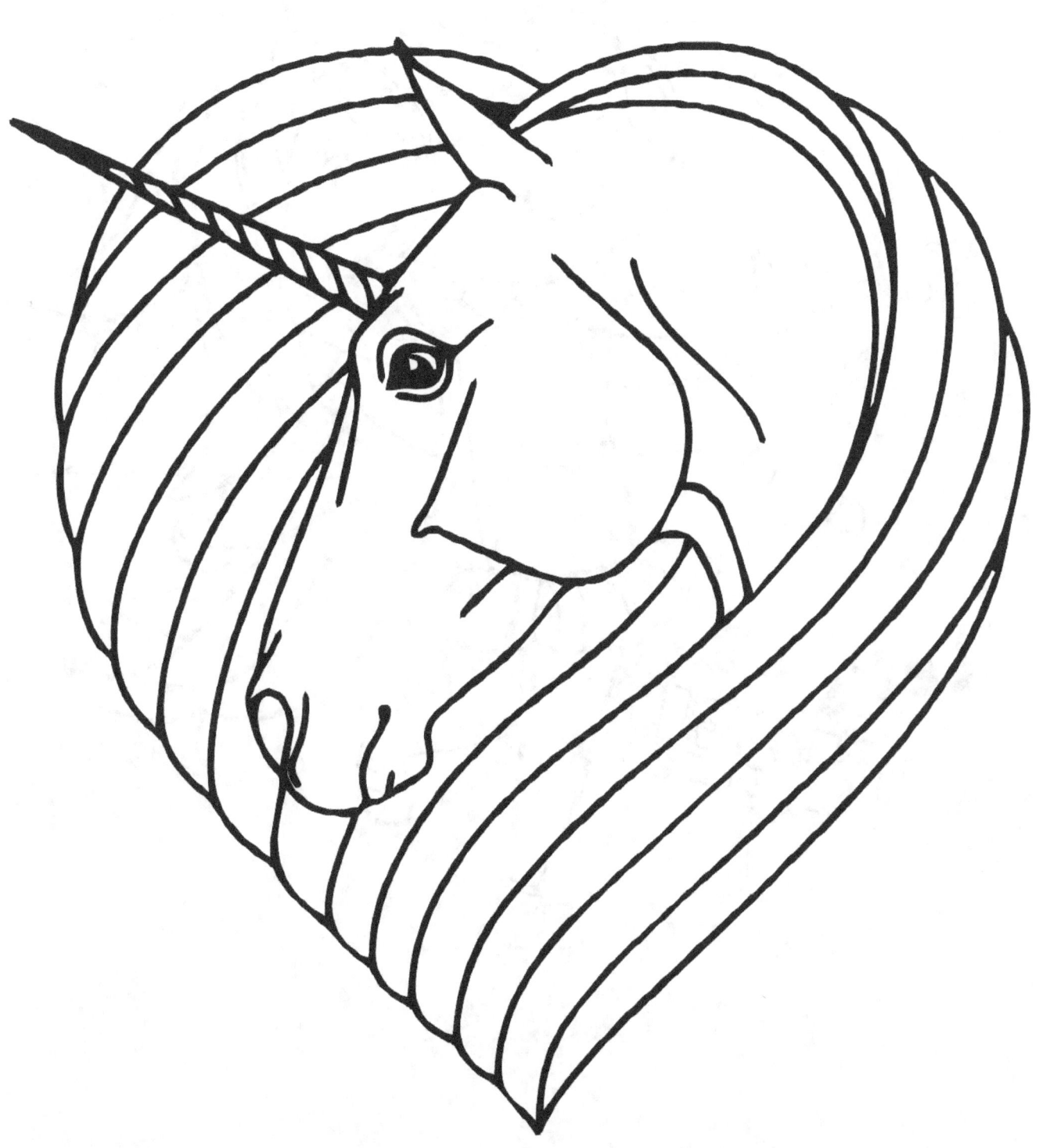

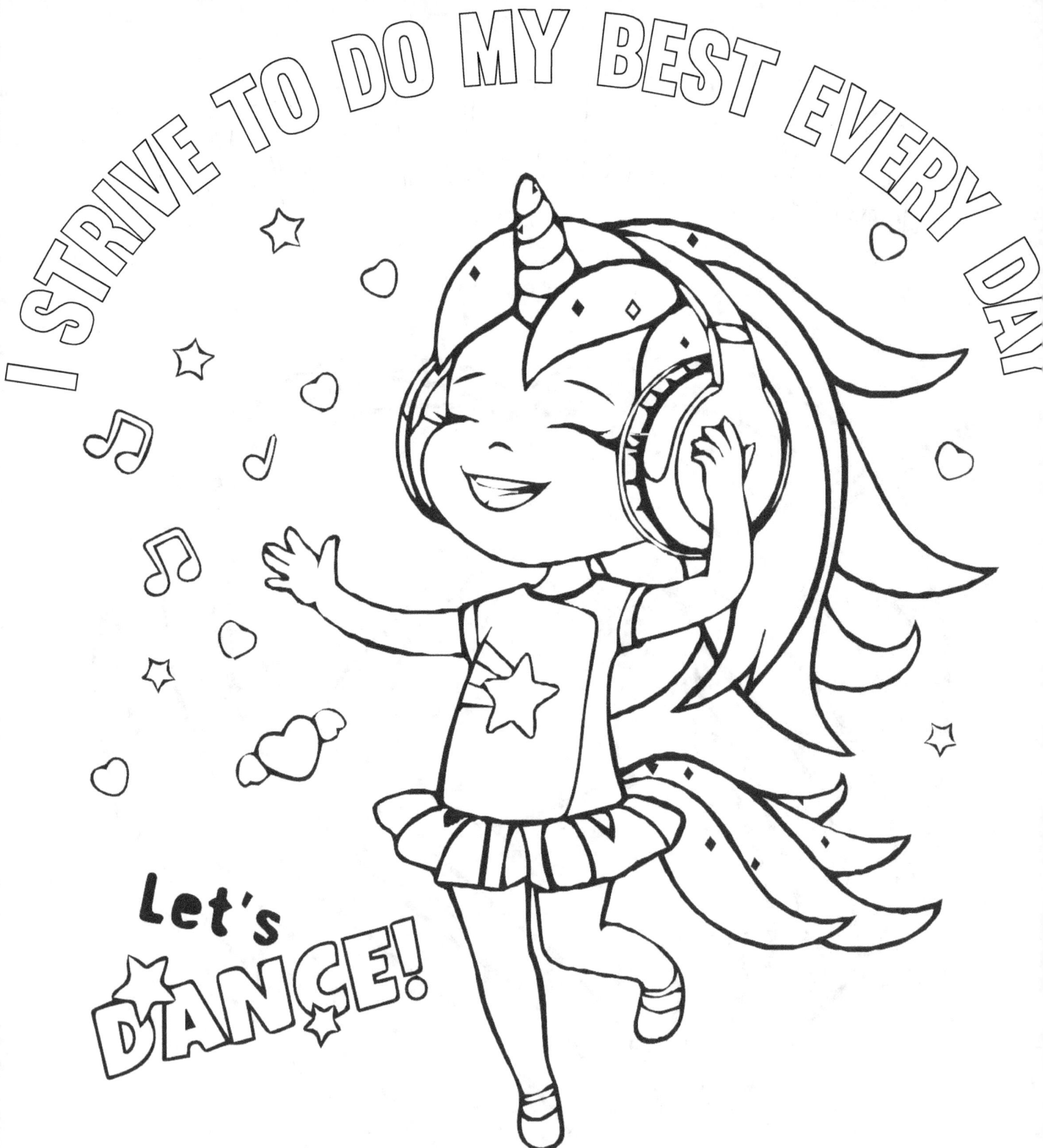

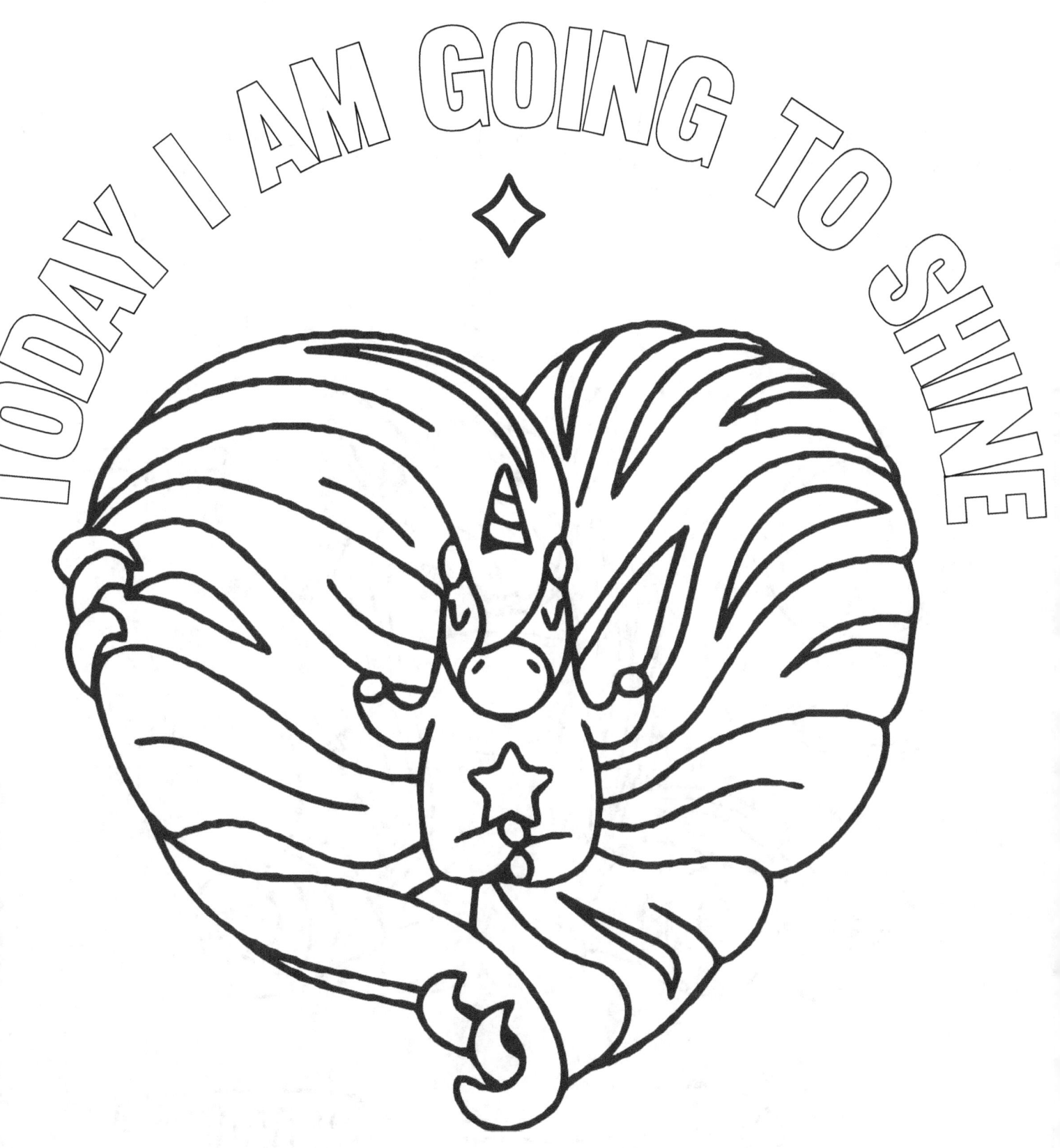

I AM SMART

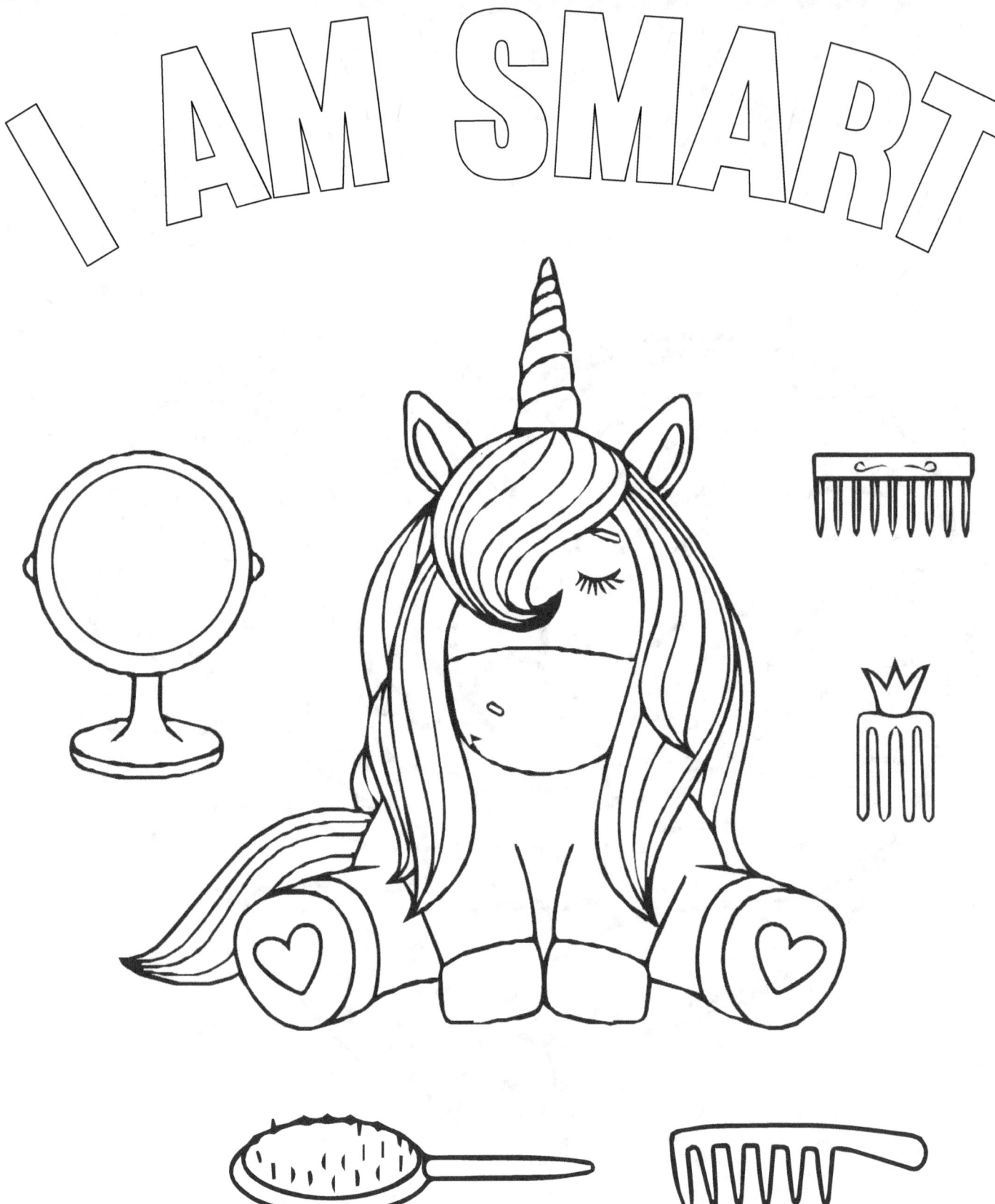

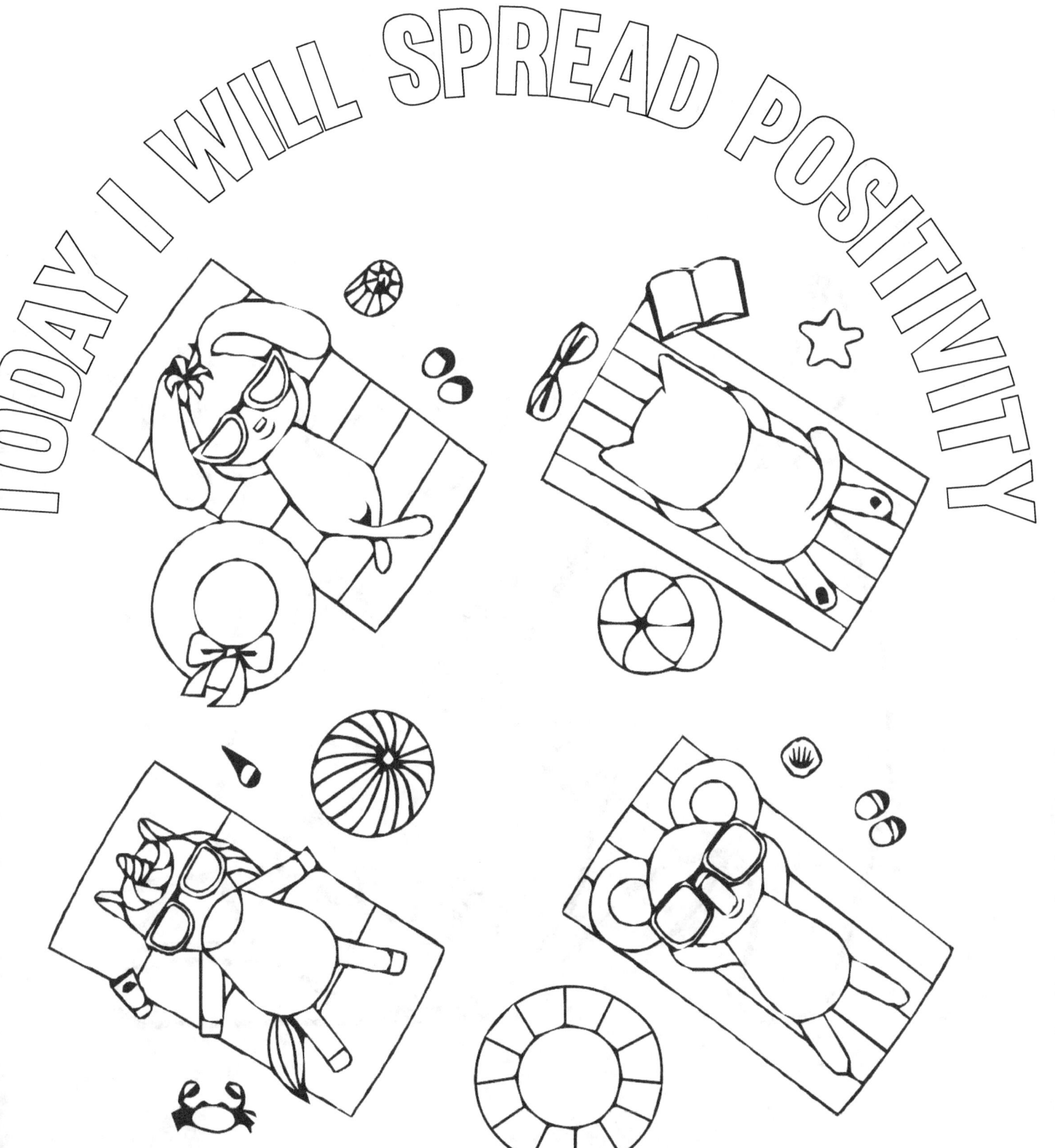

I'M NOT BEAUTIFUL LIKE YOU. I'M BEAUTIFUL LIKE ME

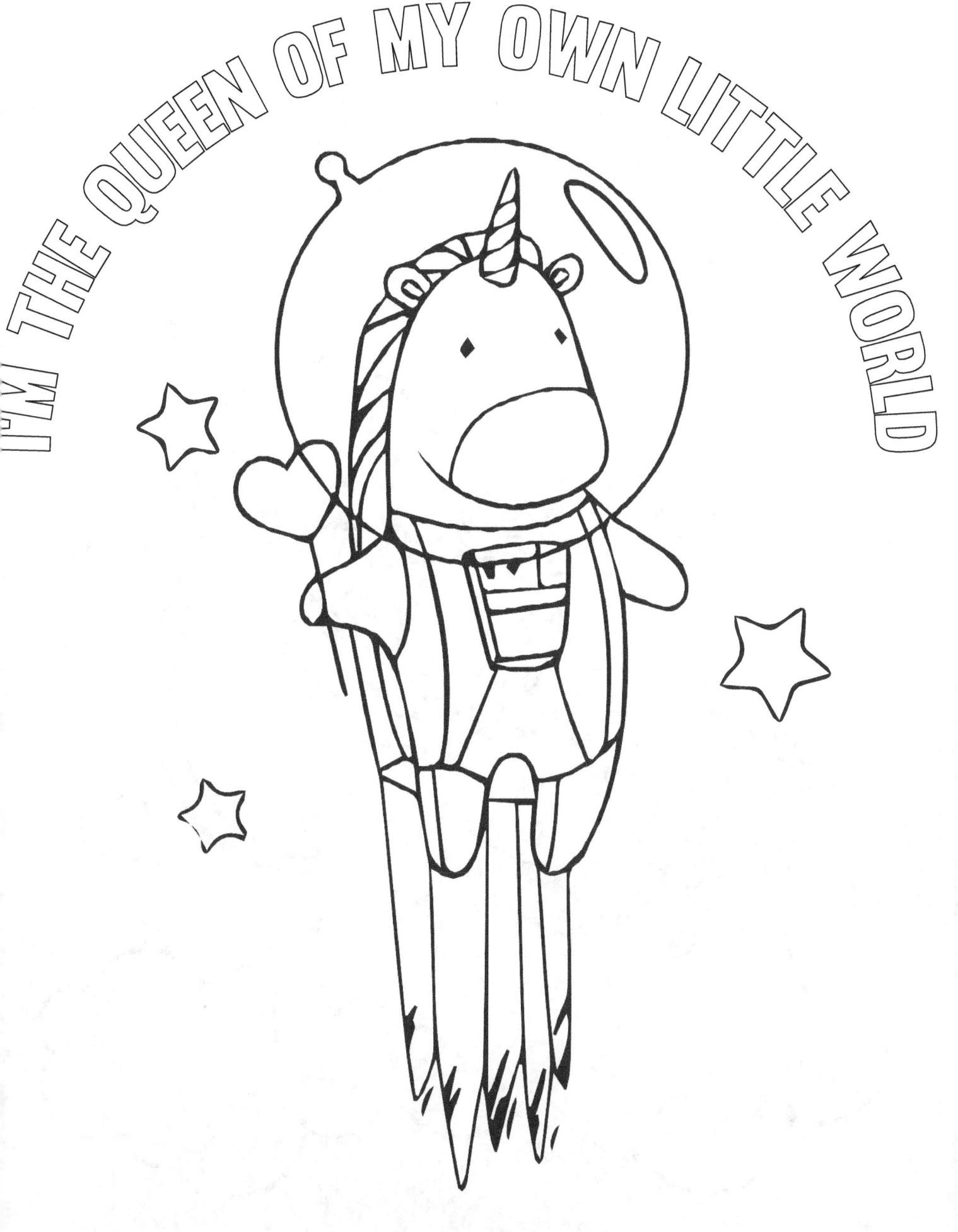

I BELIEVE IN ME

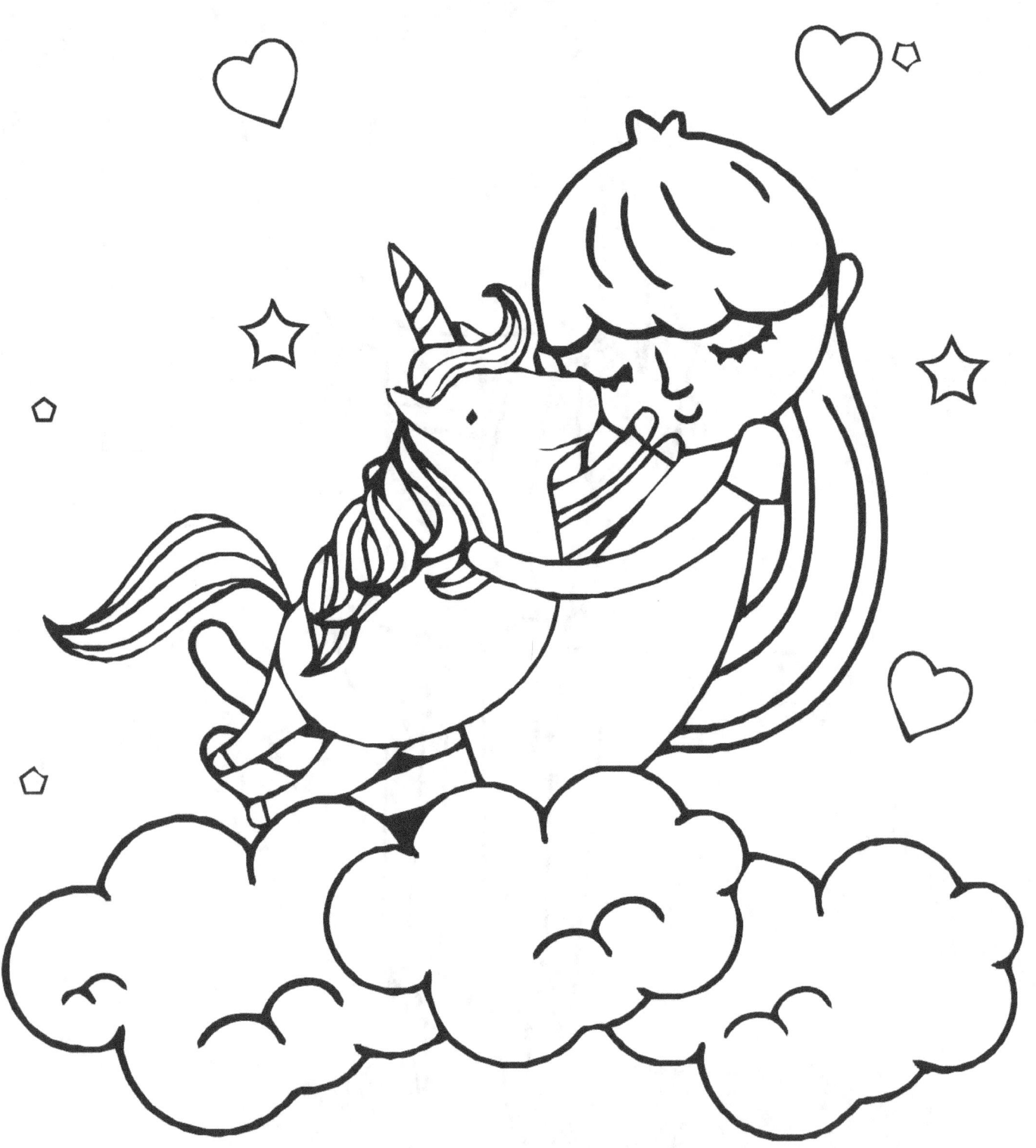

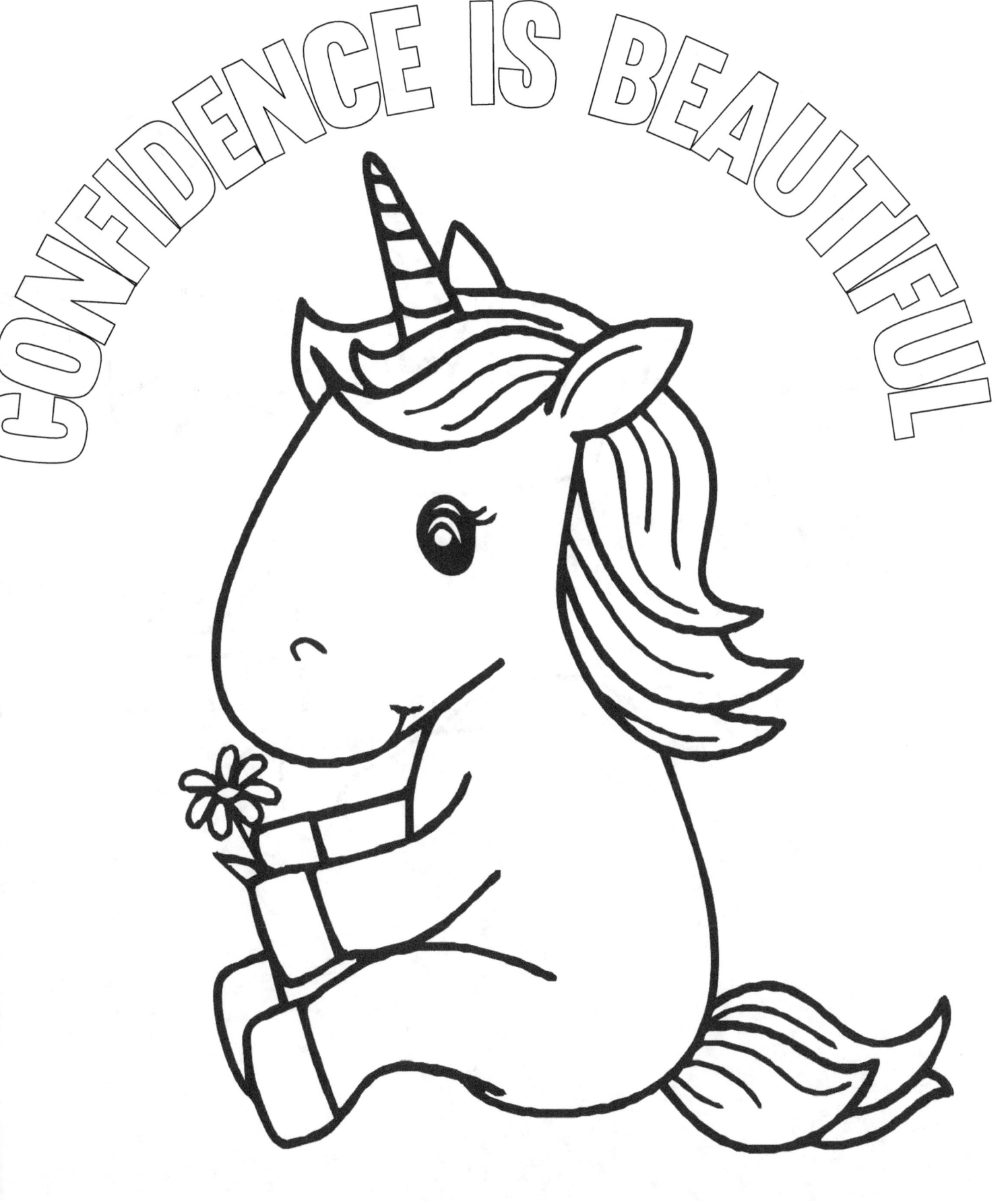

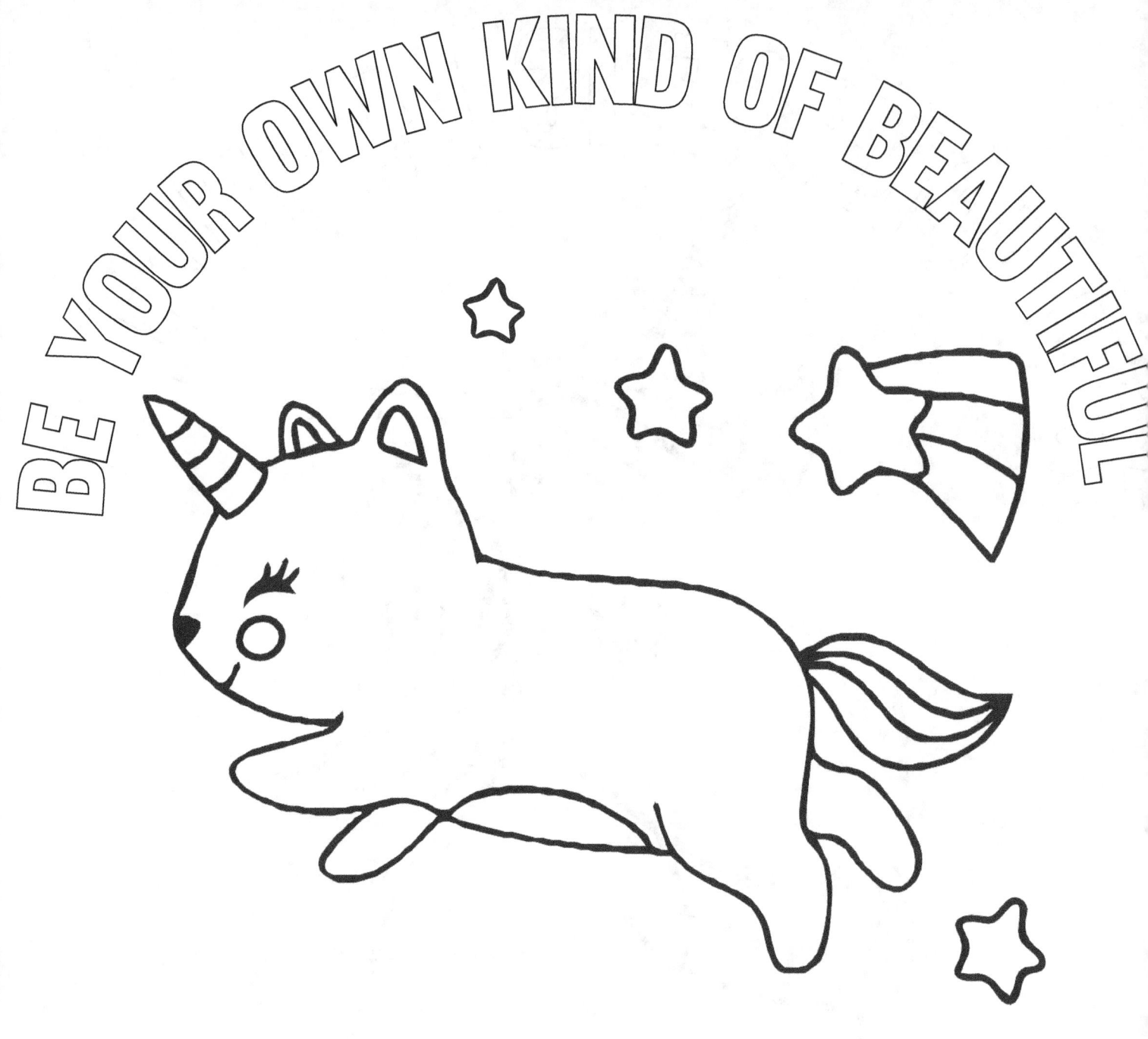

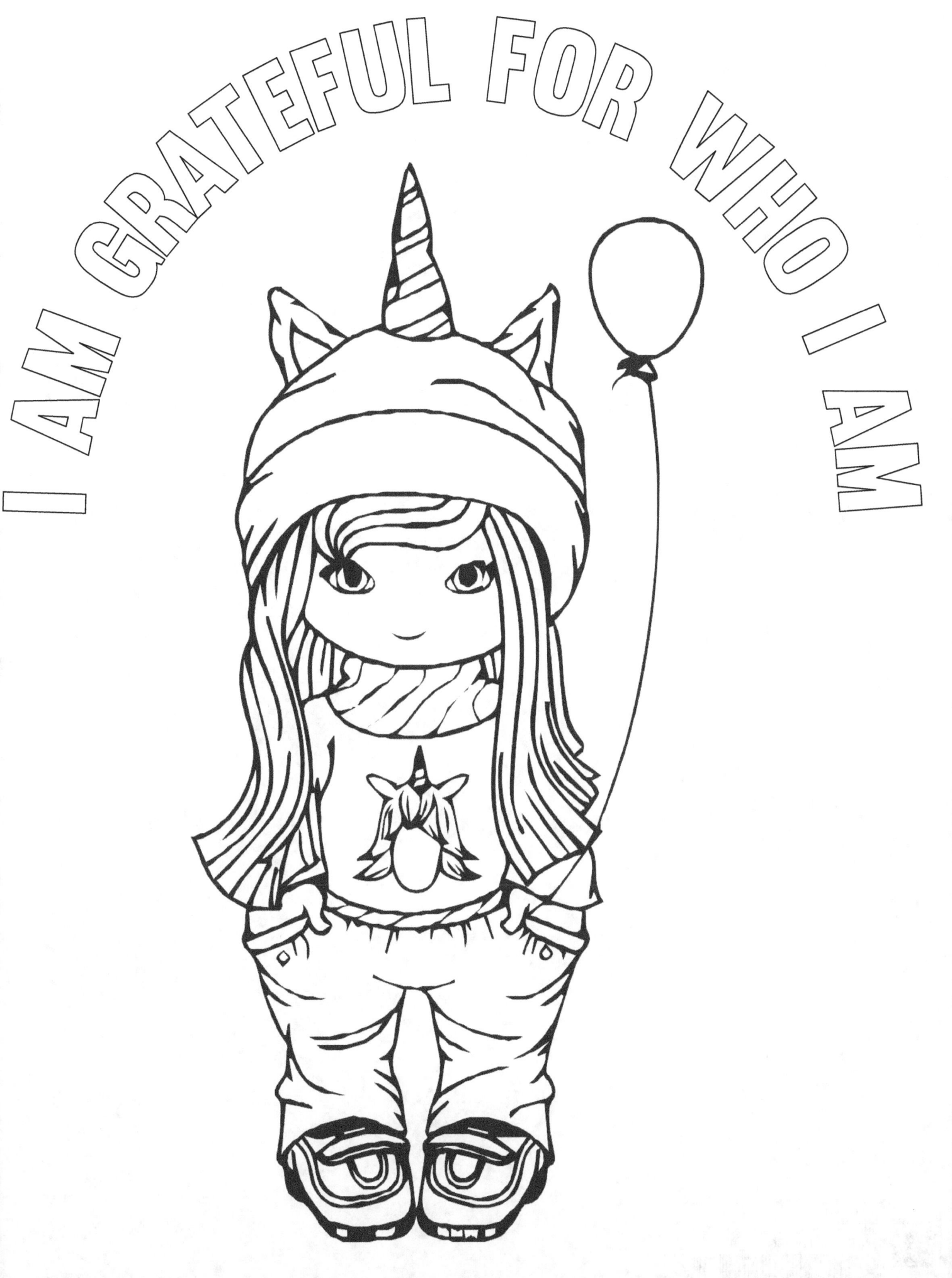

www.ingramcontent.com/pod-product-compliance
Lightning Source LLC
Chambersburg PA
CBHW080625220526
45467CB00011B/3368